Operating Principles
of the Larger Foundations

By JOSEPH C. KIGER

RUSSELL SAGE FOUNDATION
New York ~ ~ *1954*

WM. F. FELL CO., PRINTERS
PHILADELPHIA, PA.

Contents

Preface by F. Emerson Andrews 5

Introduction 9

1. Why Foundations Were Created 15

2. Diversity of Operation 26

3. The Function of a Foundation 45

4. Freedom of Action 67

5. The Public Trust 85

6. Evaluation and Conclusion 106

Appendices

    A. Statistical Information Regarding 54 Larger
       Foundations. 122

    B. Questionnaire Submitted by the Select Commit-
       tee to the Larger Foundations 127

    C. Bibliography. 138

Index 143

Preface

THE FOUNDATION as an American institution is largely a development of the twentieth century. Charitable trusts, usually small and for fixed and often narrow purposes, are nearly as old as history, but they lacked the special ingredient which makes the modern foundation dynamic—wide freedom of action.

Although the names of many of the larger foundations are now household words and the public is vaguely aware of some of their major accomplishments, little ordered knowledge concerning them is available. True, most of the major foundations issue annual reports, and in the past several years a number of histories of individual foundations have appeared. But few attempts at a broader view have been made. The bibliography included in this study lists the more important source material, but the sources are regrettably fragmentary.

Broad, scholarly studies are lacking, and are needed. Foundations are an important force operating on the forward edges of research and discovery—in medicine, in the physical sciences, and in social advance. Their importance does not lie in vast sums presumably at their disposal; their spendable income is small in today's economy, and in many areas relatively smaller than it was thirty years ago. But they are the only giver able to devote full time to learning how to give effectively, and often endowed with at least a chartered immortality.

Two comprehensive congressional investigations of foundations have been undertaken, the Industrial Relations Hearings of 1915 and the Select (Cox) Committee to Investigate Foundations Hearings in 1952. (A third investigation, under the Reece Committee, is getting under way as this book goes to press.) A wealth of new material on foundations became available in the Hearings of the Cox Committee and in the documentation the Committee had collected. As the Hearings came to a close we inquired about the availability of this material as partial background for a broad study of the administration of foundations that Russell Sage Foundation was contemplating. The data were open to inspection, and that study is now progressing.

Meanwhile we learned that Joseph C. Kiger, director of research for the Cox Committee, had in mind a special study of the development of "foundation doctrine" based largely on the material from foundations and their critics which was passing through his hands. The subject seemed promising. Many foundations have shown an obvious progression from a stage where they were mere channels for the personal giving of the donor, often largely of a relief character, to a maturer consideration of the causes of personal and social disaster, methods of cure, means of prevention, and ways of building strength and creative opportunity into the lives of men and the fabric of society. Too, a historical study of foundations might show evidence of other developments—for example, a tendency to shift from "bricks and mortar" and fixed endowment programs toward special projects and research; or perhaps emphasis on medicine and the physical sciences giving way to some degree to the developing social sciences.

After the Hearings closed and the Cox Committee came to an official end, Dr. Kiger agreed to undertake his study in intellectual history under the auspices of Russell Sage Foundation as a part of our general program of philanthropic research. Consent for Dr. Kiger's use of the material was obtained from Representative Brooks Hays, acting chairman of the Select Committee to Investigate Foundations after the death of Congressman Cox, and from Harold M. Keele, general counsel to the Cox Committee. In the book that follows Dr. Kiger has made extensive use of the files and the Hearings of the Cox Committee, and earlier sources. He has consulted with members of the Foundation staff and others, but the views expressed are his own.

Joseph C. Kiger earned his undergraduate degree at Birmingham-Southern College, and his doctorate in history at Vanderbilt University. He taught history at the University of Alabama and Washington University (St. Louis). His intensive introduction to foundations began with his employment in 1952 to direct research for the Select Committee to Investigate Foundations. It was a brief assignment, but perhaps unexampled in opportunity for study of foundation developments. He supplemented the knowledge there gained by more general studies in the spring of 1953 with this project in mind. He is now a staff associate of the American Council on Education.

The Foundation joins Dr. Kiger in expressing thanks to Representative Brooks Hays and the other members of the Select Committee to Investigate Foundations, to Harold M. Keele, the Committee's general counsel, to other individuals who gave assistance in the course of this study, and to the Library of Congress.

F. EMERSON ANDREWS
Studies in Philanthropy
Russell Sage Foundation

December, 1953

Introduction

SOME fifty years have passed since the emergence of the large American philanthropic foundation as a definite and important part of our social and intellectual life. The nineteenth century saw the creation of several relatively large foundations; however, they were isolated and were the forerunners of their twentieth-century progeny.

There have been various works dealing with the history of individual foundations and with certain aspects of foundation activity. In addition, there have been various studies of a statistical and sociological nature concerning foundations. No attempt, however, has been made to provide a systematic, historical interpretation of twentieth-century foundation thought regarding the various principles that have evolved as the result of foundation planning and operation.[1] Various reasons account for this lack:

1. The inherent difficulty in treating so elusive a subject.
2. The relative newness of the large American foundation.
3. Consciousness on the part of many foundation officials that foundations are by their very nature an experimental and fluctuating force; hence their reluctance to state principles.
4. The relative paucity of published material dealing with foundation accomplishment, which is primarily due to a feeling on

[1] With the possible exception of Frederick P. Keppel's *The Foundation:* Its Place in American Life, published in 1930. Macmillan Co., New York.

9

the part of foundations that they should not boast of their achievements.

The last point is illustrated in the reply of Rockefeller Foundation officials to a government questionnaire which asked, in part, for a detailed statement of accomplishments of the Foundation:

> Before answering the group of questions in Section E about the work of The Rockefeller Foundation in several important fields, it may be useful to comment on the delicate question of claiming credit, on behalf of a philanthropic foundation, for work which is accomplished with foundation assistance. The Rockefeller Foundation has been reluctant to seek or to claim credit and would deeply regret any necessity for doing so by way of self-justification. The Foundation has sought to promote the well-being of mankind throughout the world; in doing so, it has sought ways and means of giving aid and encouragement to others who have the ability and opportunity to accomplish significant things. The Foundation can use its funds to help construct a giant telescope, but it is the genius of the men who know how to use the instrument which pushes back the frontiers of human knowledge. We can provide funds for fellowships, but it is the high quality of the work of the fellows themselves which measures the contribution to the well-being of mankind. . . . While the Foundation accepts full responsibility for its own actions, it does not wish to assert claims of a sort which would not accord with the spirit of our collaboration or with the tradition of modesty wisely established by our founders and past leaders. We are ready to state what we have done, but much of the assessment of its worth must be left to others.[1]

This book, therefore, is an attempt to supply a concise account of the various principles which have actuated foundations. In identifying these principles, comments and observations are valuable, but an irrefutable means is citation of prac-

[1] Rockefeller Foundation, *Answers to Questionnaire* Submitted to the Larger Foundations by the Select Committee to Investigate Tax-Exempt Foundations and Comparable Organizations. File Clerk's Office, House of Representatives, Washington, 1952, pp. 78–79.

Unless otherwise noted, individual foundations will be cited by reference to the page numbers of the foundation's *Answers to Questionnaire.* Summaries of the answers of several foundations will be cited by referring to the respective sections, with question numbers, of the Questionnaire. A copy of it will be found in Appendix B.

tices. The basic premise of this work, then, will be identification of principles by reference to practices.

In attempting to distill approximately fifty years of foundation thinking and practice, certain definitions and limitations had to be set.

In a general way, what is a foundation? A leading contemporary authority on the subject has defined it thus:

> A foundation may be defined as a nongovernmental, nonprofit organization having a principal fund of its own and established to maintain or aid social, educational, charitable, or other activities serving the common welfare.[1]

Organizations falling within this general definition may, according to the same authority, be divided into five or six subclassifications or types.

First, there is the general research type of foundation whose names are household words to the American people, Rockefeller, Carnegie, Ford. Foundations in this group often have substantial assets.

Second, is the special purpose foundation. Many such foundations are small.

Third, the family foundation, which is mainly differentiated from type one in that it serves as an instrument for current giving and the donor is usually living. Development into the general research type is common if the assets involved are substantial.

Fourth, the corporation foundation; established by a corporation rather than a private donor or donors but devoted to the same philanthropic purposes.

Fifth, community trusts; usually much more restricted in geographical scope and range of activity than the other types. Some, by accumulating a great many small sums, have achieved considerable size.

Finally, although not falling within the definition above, there is the National Science Foundation, established by the United States government. This type is a newcomer and pro-

[1] Andrews, F. Emerson, *Philanthropic Giving*. Russell Sage Foundation, New York, 1950, p. 90.

vides a channel for government funds to various areas of research.[1]

This study will be confined to the first three of these types, with emphasis on the first, or general, type. It will analyze only those American foundations created and operating in the twentieth century. Earlier American foundations have few, if any, of the characteristics of those created in this century. Also, their comparative number and size make them relatively inconsequential.

With a few exceptions, only those foundations whose assets total ten million dollars or more fall within the purview of the work. The emphasis will not be on what the foundations did or did not accomplish during the period under study, but rather on the development of basic principles or practices.

Government documents dealing with foundations and foundation writings and reports form by far the largest source material in this study. The previously cited *Hearings Before the Select Committee to Investigate Tax-Exempt Foundations and Comparable Organizations*, held in Washington in the fall and winter of 1952, are a mine of information. The *Answers to Questionnaire*, also previously cited, supplied by 54 of the larger foundations are particularly valuable.[2] Although the Questionnaire and the Hearings reflect their primary design to delve into the possibility of subversive activity on the part of the foundations, they also are a compendium of opinion on past and present foundation philosophy. They are unique and significant in that, prior to their compilation, a body of factual material dealing with the thought of relatively all the larger American foundations simply did not exist.

The annual reports of the various Carnegie and Rockefeller foundations were invaluable as an unfolding account of foundation development. They provided continuity that is extremely helpful in tracing nuances of thought in this intellectual history.

[1] *Hearings Before the Select Committee to Investigate Tax-Exempt Foundations and Comparable Organizations.* U. S. House, 82d Congress, 2d Session. Government Printing Office, Washington, 1953. Statement of F. Emerson Andrews, pp. 24-30.
[2] See Appendix A for brief statistical information regarding each of the foundations.

Secondary materials included observations and studies made by foundation officials and others closely connected with foundations.

This emphasis upon foundation sources was dictated by the scarcity of other informed opinion. As one observer stated in 1935: "The most amazing thing about foundations is that so few people—even informed and intelligent people—know about them."[1] That this opinion still holds true today is attested by an analysis of information-seeking letters sent out by the 1952 House Select Committee. These letters, requesting opinions and views concerning American foundations, were sent to a hundred leaders in education, business, labor, religion, and government. They were addressed to men and women who, it was felt, should be extremely well informed. Approximately one-third did not reply. Approximately two-fifths of those replying made comments that were so vague as to be of no value, or stated that they knew little about the foundations and declined to express an opinion. The others, in varying degrees, expressed cogent opinions. Where pertinent, they have been utilized in this study.[2]

The author is grateful to the members of the House Select Committee to Investigate Foundations, particularly its chairman, the late Representative E. E. Cox, Brooks Hays, acting chairman of the Committee, and Representative Richard M. Simpson, ranking Republican member, for permission to use the files of the Committee.

The Library of Congress was most helpful in providing a special study room and research aid.

Finally, the writer thanks those individuals who aided him in this work. He is particularly indebted to Harold M. Keele, counsel to the Select Committee, who has critically read the manuscript.

[1] Lester, Robert M., "The Philanthropic Endowment in Modern Life," *South Atlantic Quarterly*, vol. 34, January, 1935, p. 4.

[2] *Letters from Various Individuals* Solicited by the Select Committee to Investigate Tax-Exempt Foundations and Comparable Organizations. File Clerk's Office, House of Representatives, Washington, 1952. Unpublished.

A few of these letters were included in an appendix to the published *Hearings*.

Why Foundations Were Created

A HISTORICAL study of the principles that actuate foundations must necessarily concern itself with causation. Why were foundations created? What were the motives of the individuals who created them? These are root questions.

Although the American philanthropic foundation is in many ways a unique social development, it has deep roots in the past. Ernest V. Hollis asserts that organizations vaguely similar to modern foundations appear almost as early as any degree of civilization.

> Fourteen hundred years before the Christian era the Pharaohs of Egypt were thus setting aside funds in perpetuity. Inscriptions show contracts wherein the Pharaoh is the donor of specified kinds and amounts of wealth to a college of priests who, for a designated portion of the income, obligated their order to use the remainder to keep the tomb perpetually protected and the religious ceremonies observed. . . . The Chaldean civilization had almost identical practices as is shown by a clay tablet, dated 1280 B.C., reciting how King Marouttach bought certain lands from his vassals, built a temple on it, dedicated the whole to the god Marduk, and endowed a college of priests to operate it.[1]

[1] Hollis, Ernest V., "Evolution of the Philanthropic Foundation," *Educational Record*, vol. 20, October, 1939, pp. 575–576.

Similarly, the Greeks and Romans adopted these means in perpetuating certain ideas.[1]

The principle upon which these foundations were established was religio-ideological; they were primarily designed to perpetuate the ideas or memory of the individual setting them up. There is little indication that they were created primarily to benefit mankind.

The advent of Christianity with its basic tenet of "Love one another" saw the emergence of a deeper concern for the well-being of one's fellowman. This concept created a new chapter in the foundation motivation; indeed, it is the continuing evolution of this principle that results in our modern foundation. Thus, probably because this new principle was "in the air," even various pagan Roman emperors prior to Constantine gradually began to shift the emphasis of the foundations they created from mere attempts to perpetuate their names to well-conceived plans for the alleviation of some of the suffering in the Roman Empire. In the early part of the fourth century, Constantine, the first Christian emperor, decreed that all public and private giving should be channeled through the Christian Church.

Function and agency were united; henceforth throughout the medieval period the Christian Church can be viewed as one large foundation devoted to the spiritual and physical well-being of its communicants.

Various attempts to see that the Church made proper use of the wealth which it administered served to strengthen it as the primary and even sole means of philanthropy. For instance, in the sixth century, Justinian's *Corpus Juris Civilis* promulgated certain legal safeguards regarding the operation of charitable bequests under Church supervision. The chief effect of these was to accelerate the Church's receipt of philanthropic funds.

The purposes for which this relatively large amount of surplus wealth was to be distributed were a mixture of the spiritual and religious, physical improvement and palliation. Motives were also a mixture of these same factors, although

[1] Much of the background material here is based on data from Hollis' article, just cited, and from William A. Orton's "Endowments and Foundations," *Encyclopaedia of the Social Sciences*, vol. 5, 1931, pp. 531–537.

concern for one's soul appears to have been more persuasive than sympathy for one's fellowman. Since the Church was fundamentally a spiritual organization, in its creation and administration of bequests it emphasized the spiritual aspect of philanthropy at the expense of the alleviation of temporal woes.

Out of this situation developed two major problems. The first revolved around the relative merits of religion versus the practical, physical alleviation of suffering, and the apparent attitude of the Christian Church to favor the former. The second grew out of the Church's relative monopoly on philanthropic funds. In England, positive action was to be taken on both.

Prior to the Norman conquest, England acquiesced in the prevailing medieval principles of philanthropy. After 1066, however, England stirred restively. First, the Norman kings rejected the idea that philanthropic holdings were the sole concern of the Church and outside the purview of secular authority. Second, and perhaps more important—although a great deal less tangible—a different idea concerning philanthropy had been developing in the English mind. In particular, Englishmen were questioning the relative merits of the primarily religious or spiritual emphasis in the creation of bequests and the dispensing of charities.

William Langland illustrates this development in *The Vision of Piers the Plowman*. This poem, which is similar to Chaucer's *Canterbury Tales*, allegorically paints a description of social life and thought in fourteenth-century England. Merchants were advised that they would escape punishment and receive the Church's reward if they saved their profits:

> Therewith to build hospitals, helping the sick,
> Or roads that are rotten full rightly repair,
> Or bridges, when broken, to build up anew,
> Well marry poor maidens, or make of them nuns,
> Poor people and pris'ners with food to provide,
> Set scholars to school, or some other crafts,
> And relieve the religious, enhancing their rents;—[1]

[1] Langland, William, *The Vision of Piers the Plowman*. Translated into modern English by W. W. Skeat. Chatto and Windus, London, 1931, p. 114.

Approval of the good works principle and a questioning of religious forms are evident here.

As long as the fabric of universal Christendom held together, however, there was no significant change in the method of philanthropy. The advent of Henry VIII to the throne of England in 1509, thereforc, is significant philanthropically as well as religiously and politically. For, in confiscating the holdings of the Roman Catholic Church in the 1530's, King Henry not only broke the religious but also the foundation pattern. First, the Church monopoly of getting and giving was broken. Second, and more important, emphasis upon alleviation of man's discomfort here on earth received royal approval.

In the reign of Queen Elizabeth this underlying intellectual ferment regarding the whole question of philanthropic purposes comes to the surface. For in the forty-third year of her reign the Statute of Charitable Uses was enacted. In spelling out directly or indirectly those uses which were considered good, it clearly portrayed a concern with secular affairs. The wording is strikingly like that of *The Vision of Piers the Plowman*[1] from which we have already quoted:

> Some for relief of aged, impotent and poor people, some for maintenance of sick and maimed soldiers and mariners, schools of learning, free schools, and scholars in universities, some for repair of bridges, ports, havens, causeways, churches, sea-banks and highways, some for education and preferment of orphans, some for or towards relief, stock or maintenance for houses of correction, some for marriages of poor maids, some for supportation, aid and help of young tradesmen, handicraftsmen and persons decayed, and others for relief or redemption of prisoners or captives, and for aid or ease of any poor inhabitants concerning payments of . . . taxes.[2]

Thus emerges a basic motivating principle: promotion of the well-being of mankind; but note the practical, nonritualistic emphasis in connection with this principle.

[1] This relationship was pointed out by Henry Allen Moe in the John Simon Guggenheim Memorial Foundation's *Answers to Questionnaire*, pp. 265–270.

[2] Pickering, Danby, *The Statutes at Large* from the Thirty-ninth of Q. Elizabeth to the Twelfth of K. Charles II, inclusive. Printed at Cambridge University, 1763, vol. 7, p. 43.

Following this stamp of royal approval, a great number of small, narrow purpose foundations were created but very few that were wide-ranging. This is accounted for by the absence of another essential element or principle: freedom of action.

In putting an end to the Church's monopoly on foundation funds, the English appear to have swapped one form of monopoly for another: control by the Church for supervision by the State. And this proved to be continuing, for as soon as the royal supervision slackened, parliamentary supervision followed. Thus, from 1837 on there were intermittent Royal Commissions of Enquiry, four of which sat continuously for a period of eighteen years. Finally, a permanent regulatory body was established in 1860 which put all foundation activity under State scrutiny.

Few foundations of note were established in eighteenth- or nineteenth-century England. With respect to France:

> It may be noted that across the Channel, the French Republic, originally perhaps because of its critical attitude toward the Church, has exercised a most minute scrutiny over foundations, and that this is probably the reason why there are so few foundations in France, and why their role is comparatively unimportant.[1]

Nowhere among the countries of western Europe, where a secularization took place in the eighteenth and nineteenth centuries, can we find a group of organizations similar in number and size to the great foundations in the United States. And, of course, the concept was entirely foreign to the states of eastern Europe.[2]

Thus, although a basic motivational principle, concern for the well-being of mankind, was definitely enunciated and approved, the European state so circumscribed private philanthropy as to restrict the growth of any large foundations.

The American Scene

Prior to the Civil War, a few Americans, such as Benjamin Franklin and Stephen Girard, had set up foundations, but they

---

[1] Keppel, Frederick P., *The Foundation*, p. 16.
[2] *Hearings*, Statement of Vannevar Bush, pp. 158–159; Dean Rusk, p. 498.

were limited in concept, size, and scope. It is noteworthy that the first really significant foundation in the United States grew out of a bequest by an Englishman, James Smithson, in 1829. It can also be noted that his creation, the Smithsonian Institution, although established in 1846, is still performing a great social and educational function. Smithson's bequest of $508,000 was "for the increase and diffusion of knowledge." No one has clearly and satisfactorily explained why an Englishman, in the early part of the nineteenth century, should found a philanthropic institution, with such broad powers, in a still predominantly backwoods United States. Could it be that Smithson was motivated by a concern for his fellowman and wished to exercise that concern free from hampering, entangling, governmental restrictions?

Not until after the holocaust that was the Civil War do we get the forerunners of the large twentieth-century American foundations. Prompted by a deep concern for the plight of the stricken South, the Slater and Peabody Funds are at one with the great foundations of the twentieth century. As one writer notes, in comparing them to later foundations:

> There are at least four reasons why these national benefactions are in a class by themselves. First, the unit by which they measure their bounty is a million of dollars. . . . In the second place, in every case the donor has made the gift totally without religious or ecclesiastical conditions. The third noteworthy distinction is that the scope of each foundation is national or world-wide rather than sectional or local. The fourth distinguishing characteristic is that the conditions governing the administration of the trust funds are in each case general in character, and provision is made for future modifications as conditions change.[1]

The third and fourth characteristics will be discussed in succeeding sections. The points to be noted here are: (1) For the first time in the United States foundations with great amounts of capital have been established. (2) Religious or ecclesiastical conditions are totally absent in the creation and administration

[1] Ayres, Leonard P., *Seven Great Foundations*. Russell Sage Foundation, New York, 1911, pp. 11–12.

of these foundations. It is true that rapid accumulations of wealth in the United States following the Civil War account for the ability to create large foundations. A pondering of the second point, however, must convince one that it can only be accounted for as the logical outcome of historical development.

After the Slater and Peabody Funds, what were the immediate causes of the surge in American foundations at the turn of the century? Abraham Flexner calls the same concern for the welfare of the impoverished South which actuated Peabody and Slater the catalytic agent.[1] Too, earlier charitable bequests undoubtedly played a vital part in the creation of these foundations because they set a pattern for giving.[2] The creation in 1903 of the General Education Board is described thus:

> This Board was the result of three converging influences: Mr. Rockefeller's own generously manifested interest in the program of the American Baptist Educational Society; the activities of the Peabody Education and the Slater Funds, of which Dr. Wickliffe Rose and Dr. Wallace Buttrick, each of them later to be President of the General Education Board, respectively were officers; and finally the Southern Education Board with the opportunities for constructive help in the Southern States demonstrated by it under the leadership of Mr. Robert C. Ogden.[3]

If concern for the welfare of the South can be termed the catalytic agent in the creation of these foundations, the hand responsible for the fusion is that of Carnegie.

Andrew Carnegie's ideas in regard to foundations were not entirely new. As has been stated, the basic principle of concern for the well-being of mankind was manifest in the creation of the Slater and Peabody Funds. But Andrew Carnegie was a dramatic figure, one of the wealthiest men of his era, and con-

---

[1] Flexner, Abraham, *Funds and Foundations*. Harper and Bros., New York, 1952, pp. 1–65.

[2] Fosdick, Raymond B., *The Story of the Rockefeller Foundation*, Harper and Bros., New York, 1952; Glenn, John M., Lilian Brandt, and F. Emerson Andrews, *Russell Sage Foundation, 1907–1946*, Russell Sage Foundation, New York, 1947, pp. 3–6; Hollis, Ernest V., *Philanthropic Foundations and Higher Education*, Columbia University Press, New York, 1938, pp. 76–81; Keppel, Frederick P., *The Foundation*, p. 22.

[3] Keppel, Frederick P., *The Foundation*, p. 21.

sequently, one to be listened to by other men of wealth.[1] Furthermore, the dynamic Scotsman was a very articulate man. His *Triumphant Democracy* was published as an article in 1886, and *The Gospel of Wealth* in 1889. The basic premise of these two works was that the prevailing socio-politico-economic system was good in that it furnished a greater and greater number of people with the good things in life. This process was accompanied, however, by a corresponding increase in the amounts of surplus wealth held by a few individuals. Carnegie felt that these extremely wealthy men could do one of three things with their wealth. Leave it to heirs. Leave it for charitable purposes at death. Give it away for charitable purposes in their own lifetime. The first two he rejected as having been tried and found wanting. He concluded that the third alone affords the men of great wealth a means for its wise disposition.

Carnegie then proceeded to suit action to his words. He really got down to business when he sold his steel holdings in 1901 and started to give away three hundred million dollars. After ten years of concentrated giving, one hundred and fifty million still remained. Thereupon Carnegie set up the Carnegie Corporation of New York in 1911, which differed from the foundations he had previously established in being unlimited in purpose, with the broad aim of advancing and diffusing knowledge.[2]

In the meantime, John D. Rockefeller had written to Carnegie in a highly commendatory fashion about his philanthropic views and had indicated approval of his course of action.[3] Rockefeller began to create foundations almost as soon as Carnegie. In 1901 the Rockefeller Institute for Medical Research was established; in 1903, the General Education Board; in 1913, the Rockefeller Foundation.

Other minds had also been stirred. Mrs. Russell Sage established the foundation bearing her husband's name in 1907. Somewhat later, the Commonwealth Fund came into existence

[1] Harrison, Shelby M., and F. Emerson Andrews, *American Foundations for Social Welfare*. Russell Sage Foundation, New York, 1946, pp. 20–21.

[2] Lester, Robert M., *Forty Years of Carnegie Giving*. Charles Scribner's Sons, New York, 1941, p. 57.

[3] Keppel, Frederick P., *The Foundation*, p. 20.

through the generosity of the Harkness family. In the next three decades an increasing number of large foundations were to be formed. By the middle of the twentieth century, approximately 60 with assets of ten million dollars or more were in existence.

What principle or motive prompted these actions?

Informed opinion on this subject is varied. One writer states that there is no one explanation. He feels that foundations owe their creation to the interaction of various external and internal forces, such as the development of the capitalistic system, rapid accumulations of wealth, and the ideas of rich men. His emphasis, however, implies that the creation of foundations is largely due to impelling economic factors.[1]

Another writer emphasizes the practical reasons for the development, stemming from the difficulty of giving away large sums of money intelligently. He points out that a very wealthy man could not do it personally. This was true, even if the wealth was devoted to the simplest form of giving, that is, direct relief for the unfortunate, for the problem of professional beggars presented itself. Thus, there followed the necessity for the creation of an organization that could separate the wheat from the chaff and act as a general staff for intelligent philanthropy.[2]

In the 1930's Eduard Lindeman questioned capitalism and the profit motive, describing foundations as

> . . . symptomatic of the later and the disintegrating period of our economic development. Their existence reveals, in the first place, the fact that the vast surplus of wealth accumulated by industrialists, financiers, and speculators was not needed for purposes of reinvestment. In the second place, the rise of foundations denotes also the beginning of a rudimentary social consciousness on the part of those who accumulated the large fortunes or, if a less polite phrase is wanted, the beginning of a guilt feeling.[3]

Although giving foundation creators grudging praise in later sentences, Mr. Lindeman further states that foundations were

[1] Coffman, Harold C., *American Foundations:* A Study of Their Role in the Child Welfare Movement. Association Press, New York, 1936, pp. 15-16.

[2] Embree, Edwin R., "The Business of Giving Away Money," *Harper's Magazine*, vol. 161, August, 1930, pp. 320-321.

[3] Lindeman, Eduard C., *Wealth and Culture.* Harcourt, Brace and Co., New York, 1936, pp. 4-5.

the projection of rugged individualism into the social sphere and that their creators wanted to be able to control the redistribution of the wealth they had accumulated.

This same allegation of selfish motives has been duplicated at the present time. Apparently the main reason for its reemergence stems from the various tax laws passed in the 1940's. These laws hiked the personal and business tax rates but provided exemptions for charitable contributions. Thus, they made the philanthropic impulse very attractive in a business and tax way, and the creation of many new foundations since World War II has been attributed to them. We quote one comment:

> Donors may be primarily interested in building or conserving private fortunes, or preserving family control over finance or industry. Accumulation and immobilization of wealth in privately controlled foundations will serve these ends. Donors can give vast sums to these foundations without encountering the heavy tax burden which would otherwise accompany such transfers, and the foundations, once created, receive continuing tax benefits.[1]

An opposing viewpoint emphasizes the idealistic, semireligious motive or principle in the establishment of the large foundations. It is admitted that a desire for publicity or self-perpetuation may enter into the picture. Too, the tax exemption feature is noted:

> . . . but no one who has examined closely the beginnings of many modern foundations is likely to escape one conclusion: most of the founders were seized by a social vision which stirred them deeply, and which was in many instances a modern expression of religious feeling.[2]

Opinions that ascribe the creation of the large foundations to economic forces, the guilt feeling, or sheer expediency overlook the *Zeitgeist* in which they were predominantly created.

[1] "The Modern Philanthropic Foundation: A Critique and a Proposal," *Yale Law Journal*, vol. 59, February, 1950, p. 479. See also Eaton, Berrien C., Jr., "Charitable Foundations, Tax Avoidance and Business Expediency," *Virginia Law Review*, vol. 35, November, 1949, pp. 809–861, and December, 1949, pp. 987–1051; Lasser, J. K., "Why Do So Many Business Men Start Foundations?" *Dun's Review*, vol. 57, February, 1949, pp. 15–17, 35–44.

[2] Harrison, Shelby M., and F. Emerson Andrews, *American Foundations for Social Welfare*, p. 23. See also Keppel, Frederick P., *The Foundation*, p. 18, and *Philanthropy and Learning*, Columbia University Press, New York, 1936, pp. 7–8.

Prior to the 1940's, United States tax laws provided no compelling reasons for the creation of large foundations. Furthermore, at least until the depression of the 1930's there was relatively little questioning of the American capitalistic system. Other definitions to the contrary, this system is more than a mere economic term; involved are political, social, and ethical values that present a mystic whole. Without going into all the ramifications of this system, for present purposes, two ethical beliefs that were and still are widely and firmly held should be noted: first, it is morally proper for the individual to amass as much wealth as possible; second, it is the moral right of individuals to dispose of this amassed wealth as they desire.

In this context, one simply cannot find a compelling economic or political reason for the establishment of these foundations unless one visualizes them as the Machiavellian creation of far-sighted men attempting to pass or transfer economic and concomitant political and social power. The question arises: to whom were they attempting to transfer it and for what purposes? Certainly, some of the children of the donors are still included among Boards of Trustees, but that is not a satisfactory answer since many had no children. Besides, in most instances where children of donors are board members they do not constitute a voting majority.

To ascribe a desire to mold the future in a conservative or liberal shape, as a reason for creation, gets one off on a tortuous road that can end where one wills.

The effects of the passage of the tax laws of the 1940's have probably been overemphasized in foundation development. Surely wealth, if spurred by necessity, could find a more propitious means of perpetuating itself than devoting itself to philanthropic and humanitarian purposes.

The following conclusions appear evident: (1) American foundations are the result of the capitalistic system which, contrary to its European counterpart, allowed neither Church nor State a monopoly on philanthropic activity. (2) They were motivated by a concern for the secular well-being of mankind.

CHAPTER 2

Diversity of Operation

T HE LARGE amount of freedom ac-
corded foundations in method of establishment, types, purposes, and general means used to achieve their aims has been
fully utilized. Thus, a very healthy situation has resulted. Notwithstanding existing differences of opinion over the relative
merits of various operational procedures, there is a consensus
that these very differences are desirable in themselves.

Charters and Deeds of Trust

Methods whereby foundations are established in the United
States are an example of this diversity. Among the early foundations, the Carnegie Institution of Washington, the Carnegie
Foundation for the Advancement of Teaching, and the General Education Board were incorporated by acts of the Congress of the United States. Other foundations were set up as
charitable trusts by the wills of donors. Most, however, were
incorporated under the laws of particular states. Methods and
means used to achieve corporate status in these states also
varied widely.[1]

Charters and deeds of trust may be classified by types and by
purposes. The types are: (1) Perpetual; the donor specifies that
the principal shall be held intact forever and the income alone

---

[1] Andrews, F. Emerson, *Philanthropic Giving*, pp. 94–96.

expended. (2) Optional; the donor allows the trustees of the foundation the option as to the expenditure of principal as well as income. (3) Liquidating; the donor specifies that both principal and income shall be expended by a certain time. Many variations within these general types exist. For example, the Duke Endowment, established as a perpetuity, had a provision in its charter that restricted the expenditure of income from the endowment until the principal grew to a certain size. Many foundations of the optional type have certain administrative restrictions in their charters or deeds of trust regarding the disbursement of principal; for example, that notice be given to the trustees in advance that such action is contemplated.

Most early foundations were of the perpetual or optional type. Generally, the Carnegie group falls into the former category, the Rockefeller group into the latter category.

Julius Rosenwald departed from this pattern in the 1920's by creating the Julius Rosenwald Fund on a liquidating basis. He justified his opposition to the perpetuity characteristics of foundations by citing inequities that had arisen; for example, the church monopoly in Tudor England and the Mullanphy Fund established in St. Louis in 1851 to assist pioneers on their way west.[1]

One writer, who later became operating head of the Julius Rosenwald Fund, felt that Rosenwald's action had wide and far-reaching repercussions in chartering practices. Thus, he ascribed the creation of the Couzens Fund in 1929, on a liquidating basis, to Rosenwald's influence. Liberalizing tendencies in connection with certain Rockefeller grants are also traced to the same source and the further conclusion is drawn that "in many less conspicuous cases Mr. Rosenwald's action set a new pattern of using rather than hoarding of funds for social welfare."[2] Similar, although more cautious, comments can be

---

[1] Rosenwald, Julius, "Principles of Public Giving," *Atlantic Monthly*, vol. 143, May, 1929, pp. 599–606.

[2] Embree, Edwin R., and Julia Waxman, *Investment in People:* The Story of the Julius Rosenwald Fund. Harper and Bros., New York, 1949, pp. 31–32.

found in foundation reports and other works of the late twenties and thirties.[1]

Rosenwald's views, however, do not appear to have had an appreciable influence on the creators of large foundations. This is shown by an analysis of the 54 foundations answering the Select Committee Questionnaire. Only five of the 54 are liquidating funds. A small majority are chartered or deeded as optional foundations.[2]

The conclusions of Henry S. Pritchett appear to be more nearly correct. In an article published in 1929 he stated that any social organization had within itself the seeds of decay; unlike a business, it had no automatic profit scale by which to gauge its worthwhileness. He felt that arguments in favor of perpetuities could be based on Carnegie's reasons for favoring them: abiding faith in mankind and confidence in the continuing good judgment of trustees. He also noted that a fixed term endowment could prove a mixed blessing in forcing trustees to spend money at unpropitious times. His conclusion, however, was that each type had its place and that, in the last analysis, choice of good men would make all effective.[3] Similar views were expressed in the 1929 *Annual Report* of the Carnegie Corporation of New York.

This agreement to disagree prevails today. No one type of charter or deed of trust appears to have a monopoly on efficacy or preference. One writer sums it up this way:

> No final agreement has been reached on the relative merits of the perpetuity with its greater stability, contributing to both the present and the future but in danger of obsolescence or ineffectiveness, and the policy of liquidation, making larger sums available for a brief term.[4]

[1] Coffman, Harold C., *American Foundations:* A Study of Their Role in the Child Welfare Movement, pp. 57–58; Hurlin, Ralph G., "Trends Shown in the Establishment of Recent Foundations," *Changing Conditions in Public Giving*, edited by Alfred Williams Anthony, Abbott Press and Mortimer Walling, Inc., New York, 1929, p. 29; Maurice and Laura Falk Foundation, *Report*, 1930–1932, p. 16.

[2] *Questionnaire*, sec. A-15. See p. 128.

[3] Pritchett, Henry S., "The Use and Abuse of Endowments," *Atlantic Monthly*, vol. 144, October, 1929, pp. 517–524.

[4] Andrews, F. Emerson, *Philanthropic Giving*, p. 100.

In commenting on American foundations, one student notes that one of the chief characteristics which differentiate them from ancient charity is their variety of purposes. He observes that some cover a wide range of objectives, others are limited or restricted to aiding one geographic area or some special group or cause. He concludes that in their purposes they are as diverse as "the interests of the men who created them."[1] Bearing this out, two-thirds of the foundations answering the Questionnaire of the House Select Committee of 1952 stated that their charters or deeds of trust empowered them to engage in activities of a broad, general welfare purpose with no limitations as to locale or use. One-third were restrained as to locale or use, or both. Those whose charters or deeds of trust specified the locale invariably were created in that locale. No one section of the United States had a preponderance of these limited, local purpose foundations. They are found in New York, Texas, Colorado, Ohio, and other states.

Health and education were usually the fields designated for operation by foundations whose charters or deeds of trust specified that endowments were to be used only for certain purposes.[2]

There are wide differences of opinion on how objectives are to be reached among those foundations with broad, general purpose charters, as well as those having restrictive charters. In these foundations resources may be concentrated on a single region or a single purpose, or even an aspect of that purpose.

Approximately half of the 54 foundations that responded to the Questionnaire stated that they restricted their operations with respect to use or locale, despite the fact that two-thirds of the respondents had general or broad charters.[3]

With few exceptions, foundation opinion has preferred general or broad charters to those that are specific. It is asserted that overly specific charters or deeds of trust have been a perennial cause of complaint by foundation administrators.[4] This

[1] Coffman, Harold C., *American Foundations*, pp. 19–24.
[2] *Questionnaire*, sec. B-1. See p. 128.
[3] *Questionnaire*, sec. B-2. See p. 129.
[4] Hollis, Ernest V., *Philanthropic Foundations and Higher Education*, pp. 81–86.

feeling, admirably summarized as "trying to outguess the future,"[1] is ludricrously illustrated by the endowment whose specified purpose was to supply books for a church tower; the value of the endowment increased to the point that the book-buying income filled the church tower to overflowing.[2]

For one reason or another, some of the 54 respondents declined to state their opinions on the broad as opposed to the specific charter.[3] A few felt that it would be almost impossible to delineate exactly between a general and a specific charter; therefore, the whole matter was one of interpretation. They did feel, however, that such phrases as "diffusion of knowledge," "betterment of mankind," and so on, were too vague.[4] One foundation official suggested as a possible guide that when the life of the foundation was limited, the charter or deed of trust be specific. Conversely, when the foundation was of the perpetual or optional type, the general purpose charter or deed of trust could be utilized.[5]

A majority of the foundations, however, came out unreservedly for the general purpose charter or deed of trust.[6] Thus, the instance of the endowment to provide red flannel underwear for divinity students in Boston is cited as an example of the desirability of a general purpose charter.[7] One foundation stated that charters or deeds of trust

> . . . should not be specific. The specific type of activity designated by the founder might be completely negatived. Suppose it was limited to cancer research only and within the year a cure for cancer was found. What then? It also would prevent aid on some problem that did not exist at the time of the designation,

[1] Keppel, Frederick P., *Philanthropy and Learning*, p. 170.

[2] *Idem, The Foundation*, p. 25.

[3] Cullen Foundation, *Answers to Questionnaire*, p. 14; John A. Hartford Foundation, *Answers*, p. 10; Eugene Higgins Scientific Trust, *Answers*, p. 11; James Foundation of New York, *Answers*, pp. 33–34; Kate Macy Ladd Fund, *Answers*, p. 17; Mayo Association, *Answers*, p. 10; William Rockhill Nelson Trust, *Answers*, p. 11.

[4] Altman Foundation, *Answers*, p. 13; Samuel S. Fels Fund, *Answers*, p. 23; Godfrey M. Hyams Trust, *Answers*, p. 52; William H. Miner Foundation, *Answers*, p. 31.

[5] Carnegie Endowment for International Peace, *Answers*, p. 107.

[6] *Questionnaire*, sec. G-8. See p. 137.

[7] Andrew W. Mellon Educational and Charitable Trust, *Answers*, p. 36.

but which would be more important than the designated objective. In our community and national life we must rely upon the
sound exercise of human judgment. The same reasons support the
reliance upon the sound discretion of the governing boards of
foundations.[1]

Another maintained that since in business enterprises purpose was expressed in broad terms, the same practice should
be employed by charitable corporations.[2] Still another, in ob-
jecting to overly specific charters, held that "it would be a mistake to require exact and specific language to describe the type
of activity in which foundations may engage; first, because it
would be almost impossible to describe any activity in such
exact detail so as to leave no room for doubt; and, second, such
exacting requirements as to definition and detail would discourage the setting up of such funds."[3]

The consensus was that, in order to avoid the onus of the
"dead hand," that is, to be able to adjust to changing times
and conditions, a general purpose charter or deed of trust was
best for a philanthropic foundation.

This preference was qualified, however, by a feeling that the
degree of limitation in charters and deeds of trust was a field
where opinion and arrangements varied. Thus, creators of individual foundations would differ in their views, as would
trustees of particular foundations. Far from being a detriment
however, such diversity was viewed as beneficial. The idea or
principle lying behind this belief is, of course, that operation
under varied charters or deeds of trust tends to prevent ossifica-
tion among the foundations.

Trustees and Officers

Boards, variously titled trustees, directors, and so on, play
the policy-forming and governing role in foundation operations. Immediately beneath them in the foundation hierarchy

---

[1] Max C. Fleischmann Foundation of Nevada, *Answers*, p. 15.
[2] Association for the Aid of Crippled Children, *Answers*, p. 11.
[3] Charles Hayden Foundation, *Answers*, p. 25.

are the foundation officers: presidents, vice-presidents, directors, secretaries, treasurers, counsels, and so on.

Here again, it is hopeless to attempt to deduce a positive principle or series of principles upon which all foundations have operated in the selection of these officials, in terms of background, place of residence, and status in American society. It is true that various generalizations about desirable characteristics can be made. Keppel listed these: willingness to devote a considerable amount of time to foundation activity; in the case of an operating foundation, special knowledge in its chosen field; independence of judgment; willingness to delegate details of administration to staff.[1] Contemporary authorities concur in the foregoing qualifications and add the following: broad experience in varied fields, ability to work as a member of a team, deep concern or sympathy for the welfare of humanity.[2]

Concrete, statistical attempts have been made to analyze the characteristics of trustees. One writer, in 1936, typified the foundation trustee as

> . . . a man well past middle age; he is more often than not a man of considerable affluence, or one whose economic security ranks high; his social position in the community is that of a person who belongs to the higher income-receiving class of the population; he is, presumably, "respectable" and "conventional" and belongs to the "best" clubs and churches, and he associates with men of prestige, power, and affluence. His training has been largely in the arts and humanities and he possesses only a slight background in the sciences and technologies. He resides in the Northeastern section of the United States and has attended one of the private colleges in that region. His "intelligence" is ranked high by various institutions of higher learning from whom he has received signal honors. He receives his income primarily from profits and fees. In short, he is a member of that successful and conservative class which came into prominence during the latter part of the nineteenth and early twentieth century, the class whose status is based primarily upon pecuniary success.[3]

[1] Keppel, Frederick P., *The Foundation*, pp. 64–66.

[2] *Hearings*, Statement of Charles Dollard, pp. 327–329; Russell C. Leffingwell, pp. 372–373; Donald Young, pp. 387–388; Michael Whitney Straight, pp. 412–413; Alfred P. Sloan, Jr., p. 454; Dean Rusk, pp. 479–480.

[3] Lindeman, Eduard C., *Wealth and Culture*, pp. 44, 46.

A similar study, also published in 1936, drew essentially the same conclusions.[1]

Apropos of the remark that there are "lies, damned lies, and statistics," fallacies may arise by using mass data for the generalizations previously mentioned. A survey of individual boards may be a better method of ascertaining trustee characteristics. On this basis, it has been ascertained that what amounts to a revolution has taken place in some foundations; the original donors and the men they had gathered 'round them on the Boards of Trustees were replaced by men with a far less conservative background.[2]

A recent critic, while taking the position that the boards were still "heavily weighted toward conservatism," felt that they had not allowed their background to influence their decisions affecting foundation policy. This writer believed that there was little danger of trustees' influencing foundation policy to the right or the left. He feared that they would exert no influence at all and merely drift with shifting economic, political, and social currents.[3]

Today, decreasing interest is shown in the purely pecuniary status of foundation trustees. Two more pressing issues are the geographical distribution of trustees and whether or not they are paid for their services.

Foundations in the past have been conscious of criticism leveled at them because of an alleged concentration of "New Yorkers" or "easterners" on their boards. In 1930 the *Annual Report* of the Carnegie Corporation of New York, in a rebuttal to "the murmurings which are heard from time to time as to the dominant influence of what is called the 'New York point of view,'"[4] called attention to the noneastern background of two new members. The report concluded that the appointment of these two men would help to focus the thought of the Corporation on a national rather than a sectional basis. A 1936 re-

[1] Coffman, Harold C., *American Foundations*, p. 30.

[2] Hollis, Ernest V., *Philanthropic Foundations and Higher Education*, pp. 88–90.

[3] Embree, Edwin R., "Timid Billions: Are the Foundations Doing Their Job?" *Harper's Magazine*, vol. 198, March, 1949, pp. 28–37.

[4] Pp. 9–10.

port of the same foundation stated that "in making new appointments, greater and greater care is being exercised to enlarge the horizon of the existing Board."[1]

Although conscious of the question, foundation officials have approached it in their characteristically diverse ways. Officers of several foundations admit that a preponderance of their trustees is drawn from the New York-New England area. The reasons for this concentration are basically convenience and efficiency. They state that there are a large number of qualified people from whom to choose in this area and that there is no problem of timing or expense in getting them to New York to attend meetings. Another important factor is the frequent necessity for calling special meetings of executive or financial committees. A California or Arizona resident would be required to engage in Herculean planning in order to attend special meetings of these committees. Aside from convenience and efficiency, it is pointed out that a preponderance of trustees who are residents of the East does not preclude a truly national viewpoint, since many of them were born in or have close connections with other parts of the country.[2]

While admitting the necessity of having an executive nucleus in the New York area, another group of officials feel that a broader geographical representation is better foundation policy and is a definite factor in the selection of their trustees.[3]

Pay for trustees is not so divisive an issue as place of residence. In general, trustees are not usually paid beyond compensation incidental to meetings and other foundation business. There have been, however, outstanding exceptions. For instance, in its early years the Carnegie Corporation of New York paid its trustees $5,000 a year. The Duke Endowment has consistently given its trustees a fixed percentage of its income. Furthermore, the largest foundation in existence today, the Ford Foundation, pays its trustees $5,000 annually. A few other foun-

[1] P. 38.
[2] *Hearings*, Statement of Charles Dollard, p. 329; Donald Young, p. 387; Dean Rusk, pp. 480–481.
[3] *Ibid.*, Statement of Malcolm Pratt Aldrich, p. 407; Marshall Field, pp. 438–439; Joseph E. Johnson, pp. 576–577.

dations pay varying amounts. In addition, many have one or more trustees who occupy salaried posts within the foundation.

The thinking that lies behind payment of trustees is that planning for a large, modern foundation is a difficult, taxing job that requires a great deal of time and effort. Although believing that this work can be only partially compensated, this school holds that, in all fairness, at least a partial payment should be made. Coincidentally, it is felt that the acceptance of remuneration places a certain moral obligation on the recipient to attend meetings and devote time to other foundation business, which he might otherwise shrug off.[1]

Others believe that compensation is not a critical factor in the trustee picture, that the importance of the job to be done overrides any pecuniary consideration. Too, it is felt that men who are qualified to be trustees should accept such duties as a social obligation. Also the feeling exists that there is something abhorrent about individuals accepting a fee to give the money of others away for charitable purposes.[2] Finally, there is the danger of nepotism in this system.

Foundation literature abounds with discussion concerning the philanthropists and their cohorts, the trustees. Relatively little has been written about the "philanthropoids," the paid officers who give the philanthropists' money away.[3] Despite this paucity of information, several observations can be made. In most instances, foundations are distinguished by their remarkably small staffs. This is relatively true even in the case of the largest, the Ford, Rockefeller, and Carnegie, which operate on a global scale and in an almost bewildering variety of fields. Because staffs are small and must operate in wide fields, professional staff members should have a broad outlook and knowledge in many fields; colleges and universities have seemed the natural breeding ground for these qualities, and to

[1] *Ibid.*, Statement of Henry Ford II, pp. 224–225; Paul G. Hoffman, pp. 254–255.

[2] *Ibid.*, Statement of Charles Dollard, pp. 328–329; Donald Young, pp. 388–389; Malcolm Pratt Aldrich, p. 407; Marshall Field, p. 438; Dean Rusk, pp. 480–481.

[3] The term apparently originated with Frederick P. Keppel. See *The Foundation*, p. 58.

them many foundations have looked in recruiting staff.[1] As one foundation president expressed it:

> We want men who have had a very good education, who have had some experience in higher education, that is who have actually been in colleges or universities, who have a great deal of common sense, and who have absolute integrity and imagination.
>
> We are not too much interested in what fields they have been trained in, although we would not want to get a staff made up wholly of chemists or psychologists or sociologists.[2]

The meager data available indicate that the background and characteristics of such staff members are diverse, probably to a greater degree than is true of the trustees. Accusations of potential or actual geographical, economic, or other biases have not been brought against this group.

Backgrounds of foundation trustees and professional staff are a great deal more diversified today than yesterday. This seems to be as true in respect to the economic as to the social and political spheres. It is believed that, relatively speaking, background exerts little influence on the decisions made. Indeed, these officials may be so conscious of this background bias accusation that they consciously or unconsciously make decisions that are designed to refute it.

In conclusion, although some foundations in the past have honored it more in the breech than in the observance, the principle of diversity as regards trustees and professional staff seems to have been recognized. Increasingly, today, foundations appear to be conscious of it—especially in regard to geographical diversification. Less emphasis or concern about the purely economic background of prospective officials is being displayed.

Operating Practices

It has been said, "Somebody must sweat blood with gift money if its effect is not to do more harm than good."[3]

---

[1] Keppel, Frederick P., *The Foundation*, pp. 10–11; Lester, Robert M., "The Philanthropic Endowment in Modern Life," *South Atlantic Quarterly*, vol. 34, January, 1935, p. 9; Hollis, Ernest V., *Philanthropic Foundations and Higher Education*, p. 98.

[2] *Hearings*, Statement of Charles Dollard, pp. 326–327.

[3] Carnegie Corporation of New York, *Annual Report*, 1922, p. 19.

The preceding quotation aptly summarizes the problems that confront a foundation once it has been established and its trustees and officers named. How does one go about this business of giving money away? Again, there are no hard and fast rules, no maps or guidebooks. Operating practices of individual foundations are somewhat dependent upon the size of the foundation and the types of programs to which they are committed, but are even more influenced by the men who run them at any given time. Thus, the methods by which foundations carry out their missions are again characterized by wide diversity.

In a very general way foundations can be said to operate on either tight or loose lines. The former insist on formal applications from those seeking grants, usually in writing; in order to be considered, institutions must conform to certain predetermined standards; these foundations are unlikely to make grants out of line with their established programs of activity. The latter do not insist on all the foregoing points, and, in general, the grants are smaller. While both types have advantages and disadvantages, it can be noted that a foundation operating on loose lines has a more difficult time explaining the rationale of its operation. The exchange between Michael W. Straight, president of the William C. Whitney Foundation, and Congressmen Aime J. Forand and Richard M. Simpson at the Select Committee Hearings is exemplificative. Mr. Straight emphasized the Whitney Foundation's practice of giving small grants to small groups on a very "flexible" basis, "flexibility" applying to both the foundation and the group aided. A "flexible" group was defined as one not institutionalized or committed to a more or less perpetual way of operation. Applying the "flexibility" idea to the foundation itself raised, first, the issue of slipshod methods and, second, the possibility of collusion between grantor and grantee.[1]

An outstanding example of foundation operation on tight lines is the Rockefeller Foundation. The impetus in that direction was probably given by John D. Rockefeller himself. Creating his fortune by meticulous attention to efficiency, he

[1] *Hearings*, pp. 414–417.

thought the same methods should be applied to philanthropy. For example, prior even to the creation of this Foundation, Mr. Rockefeller stated that the best way for those seeking beneficence from him was to put their requests in writing. He added that these written presentations were given careful consideration by an expert staff and that they formed the basis for any further action.[1]

Foundations operate in different ways in respect to the type of grants made. Some make grants primarily to other institutions or agencies for general or specific projects. Others make grants (they actually pay salaries) to permanent or semipermanent members of their own staff for the performance of specified tasks. Still others make grants primarily to individual persons outside the foundation for various purposes. For convenience these may be classified as institutional, operating, and fellowship foundations, respectively. It may be well to note here that delineating foundations in these classifications is a rather arbitrary process, for very often a foundation may be actively engaged in making all three types of grants. Too, there are exceptions to be noted in nearly all cases and, significantly, such exceptions are viewed with favor, even by those foundations operating on tight lines. A 1941 report of Carnegie Corporation of New York stated:

> One of the best pieces of advice ever received and followed by the Carnegie Corporation was from Dean Gildersleeve of Barnard, namely, to set aside each year a small percentage of the income from which grants might be made without reference to consistency or precedent.[2]

Apparently the advice has been followed; for example, three of the larger institutional type of foundation still allow their principal executive officers, within monetary limitations, discretionary powers to make fellowship grants subject to later trustee approval.[3]

---

[1] Rockefeller, John D., "Some Random Reminiscences of Men and Events," *The World's Work*, vol. 17, January, 1909, pp. 11101–11110.

[2] Pp. 47–48.

[3] Carnegie Corporation of New York, *Answers*, p. 12; General Education Board, *Answers*, pp. 21–22; Rockefeller Foundation, *Answers*, pp. 29–30.

The institutional type of operation is probably the most popular and widely used. It has several advantages from a foundation standpoint. The grantee institution or group relieves the foundation, to a considerable extent, of the responsibility of evaluating and carrying through specific projects or programs. It allows the foundation to dispense a great deal of money rapidly. It counteracts a tendency toward "scatteration giving," that is, a plethora of small, ineffectual grants. It has the effect, sparked in many cases by the addition of "conditions" to the grant, of causing supplementary grants from other sources, thus augmenting the force or impact of the original grant.[1] A further consideration, and one of the utmost concern, is that of objectivity. In some quarters it has been felt that it is impossible for an operating foundation, which pays and, by implication, controls its own staff, to maintain complete objectivity. Thus, early in its career, the Rockefeller Foundation considered the creation of an operating economic division similar to the health division. This proposal evoked so great a public controversy, however, that the project was dropped, with the result that, except for direct operation in a few noncontroversial fields such as health, medicine, and agriculture, the Foundation henceforth limited itself "to grants to outside agencies competently organized and staffed to carry on the work in question. In other words, the Foundation . . . [became] primarily not an operating agency but a fund-dispensing agency." It was further explained that

. . . this new policy obviously did not imply that the Foundation would avoid controversial questions. It meant that its approach to such questions would take the form of grants to agencies independent of Foundation control. In no other way could the objectivity of research be established beyond cavil and the projects freed from suspicion of ulterior interest. This was the new pattern which the Foundation was to follow for many years to come.[2]

The operating foundations, on the other hand, list several advantages: they can develop a cumulative body of operating

[1] *Hearings*, Statement of Paul G. Hoffman, pp. 239, 253–254; Marshall Field, p. 437.
[2] Fosdick, Raymond B., *The Story of the Rockefeller Foundation*, pp. 27–28.

experience, especially, as is true in most cases, if they concentrate on a few fields; the close coordination of personnel makes
them especially competent in some research ventures; they
lend themselves to speedy shifts of emphasis, since there are no
long-range commitments to outsiders.

The fellowship foundation is generally considered the most
difficult to operate. Probably, the principal reasons stem from
the fact that this type of granting has none of the advantages
previously mentioned. There can be no delegation of responsibility for administration, or as has been stated "no subcontracting," as in the case of the institutional foundation. On the
other hand, choice of specific programs or projects is more or
less limited, and once grants are made, little guidance can be
exercised. (Attempted guidance would be a violation of the principle of the independence of the grantee, of which more will
be said later.) An additional reason was stated in 1952 by President Charles Dollard of the Carnegie Corporation of New York:

> If you are going to make grants to individuals, you have, in my
> judgment, to staff up to a much greater extent than if you are
> making institutional grants, because though it may sound absurd,
> it takes more careful study, more careful investigation to make a
> grant of $5,000 to one individual than it does to give a grant of
> a half million to a well-established university, because in one case
> you have got to get all of your facts yourself, in the other case the
> facts are very readily available, and indeed, you will start with a
> good deal of knowledge about the institution.[1]

Notwithstanding this observation, the Carnegie Corporation
has recognized the importance of this type of granting. An ex-
amination of the writings of the former president, Frederick P.
Keppel, shows, by implication, a developing interest. In 1930
he offered Zinsser's observation on research as a reason for the
lack of success in applying to other fields the cooperative research practiced in the natural and medical sciences:

> Research councils and foundations organize cooperative re-
> searches, thinking that shy truth can be snared by the noisy ad-

[1] *Hearings*, Statement of Charles Dollard, p. 350.

vance of a well-drilled company of technicians, forgetting that discovery was ever a solitary task, in which cooperation must be
spontaneous, asked, as the need arises, by one lonely seeker from
another.[1]

In various official reports, Mr. Keppel questioned the
efficacy of granting through other institutions and agencies and
concluded that, in any event, there were far too many of these
intermediate bodies. Then in 1936 he discussed the relative
merits of various types of granting and, although admitting he
did not know whether fellowship granting was gaining or losing
favor, he said that he believed that it held great possibilities.[2]
While not committing himself or the foundation to a definite
and emphasized adherence to this type of granting, two years
later he stated that, within his foundation, fellowship granting
had been growing from year to year because of satisfactory
results.

He announced that he was engaging a man to take charge of
this augmented type of granting, and that man, interestingly
enough, was Charles Dollard.[3] Finally, the next year, 1939,
Keppel came out unreservedly for fellowship granting. He
maintained that institutions tended to promote the safe and
mediocre rather than the difficult and brilliant persons. He felt
that fellowship grants should be used to combat this situation.
Therefore, the granting of fellowships was to cut across all
lines of foundation activity and Dollard was retained on a
permanent basis to head the program.[4]

The outstanding example of a pure fellowship foundation is
the John Simon Guggenheim Memorial Foundation. It de-
votes itself exclusively to making grants to individuals outside
the foundation to enable them to carry out specific projects
that the petitioners themselves propose. Applications are ac-

[1] Zinsser, Hans, *In Defense of Scholarship:* Address Before the Graduate School
of Brown University, Commencement, 1929. Brown University, Providence,
1929, p. 11. (Quoted by Keppel on p. 88 of *The Foundation.*)

[2] Carnegie Corporation of New York, *Annual Report,* 1932, p. 28; 1933, p. 19;
1936, pp. 40–41.

[3] *Ibid.,* 1938, pp. 26–29.

[4] *Ibid.,* 1939, pp. 30–32.

cepted for projects in all fields, including the humanities, social sciences, and fine arts.[1]

Conceding that a proposal or application fits into the general program of a foundation, what is the basis upon which grants are determined? In a foundation's early years, it is highly probable that the donor decided who were to receive grants.[2] In later years, what is the basis?

Question B-5 of the 1952 Select Committee Questionnaire asks for the basis upon which grants were determined. The answers to the question throw little light on the problem. All but a few are so vague that they are relatively worthless. Many probably misconstrued the question. In any event, for those giving clear and detailed answers, the following generalization may be made: Specific committees of the Board of Trustees are appointed to compare and evaluate all applications. In addition, foundation staff members make careful, on-the-spot investigations of many of the applications and make detailed written and verbal reports to the Board of Trustees or its committees. After this process has been accomplished, final determination of grants is made by the vote of the whole Board of Trustees.[3]

Foundation Investments

Writing on this subject in 1930, Keppel made the following observations: American foundations operated more efficiently in this field than their English predecessors; foundation trustees take the initiative as regards investment policies; larger foundations usually have a full-time investment officer working under a finance committee of the trustees; a reserve fund is usually built up to guard against bad investments; in general, trustees are more interested in the soundness of investments than in yield. Also, he discussed, nonconclusively, whether investments should be made for income solely or combined with an attempt to further foundation purposes.[4]

---

[1] *Hearings*, Statement of Henry Allen Moe, pp. 601–603.

[2] Embree, Edwin R., and Julia Waxman, *Investment in People*, pp. 28–29; Andrew W. Mellon Educational and Charitable Trust, *Report*, 1930–1945, p. 15.

[3] *Questionnaire*, sec. B-5. See p. 129.

[4] Keppel, Frederick P., *The Foundation*, pp. 35–38.

Sixteen years later, two authorities, covering approximately the same ground, state frankly that they will confine themselves "to certain aspects of general investment policy bearing on the special needs and purposes of foundations." Thereupon, they postulate that, in general, a conservative principle prevails of favoring investments that are secure rather than those yielding a high degree of return. They add, however, that the practice of including more common stocks in portfolios is growing. They merely phrase the question as to whether or not a foundation should invest solely for income or attempt to further implement its program by its investment policy. Concluding, Harrison and Andrews assert that antisocial investments and investments that lend themselves to accusation of undue business influence by a foundation or its officials "are unwise, not for financial reasons, but because of effects on the foundation program or reputation."[1]

With the exception of the aforementioned volumes, little has been written in this field of foundation activity. It is true that one chapter of a rather journalistic 1938 work[2] deals with the investments of the Carnegie Corporation of New York, the General Education Board, and the Rockefeller Foundation. Its conclusion seems to be that "there is no unanimity about what constitutes good investments among the foundations. . . . It even happens sometimes that one foundation is selling the same security another foundation is buying."

Only one statement concerning investments appears in the report of the Hearings conducted by the Select Committee to Investigate Foundations. This was Charles Dollard's reference to the doctrine of the prudent man, as pursued by the Carnegie Corporation of New York:

> We will not put more than 5 percent of our total investment in common stocks into any one business corporation or stock. Conversely, we will not hold in our portfolio more than 1 percent of the stock of any single business corporation. . . .[3]

[1] Harrison, Shelby M., and F. Emerson Andrews, *American Foundations for Social Welfare*, pp. 70–73.

[2] Coon, Horace, *Money to Burn:* What the Great American Philanthropic Foundations Do with Their Money. Longmans, Green and Co., New York, 1938, pp. 248–274.

[3] *Hearings*, p. 353.

The dearth of information concerning foundation investments is probably due to the fact that, with the exception of some of the older foundations, such as the Rockefeller and Carnegie, few foundations publish comprehensive reports of their financial dealings.

In the absence, therefore, of detailed, factual analysis or information on the subject of foundation investments, one can only surmise as to principles. It seems safe to assume, however, that, although some of the principles previously enunciated are followed by the foundations whose officers proclaimed them, there is great diversity in holdings and investment methods. This diversity derives in part from the varied securities given by the donors and in part from the differing characteristics of the men making up individual boards of trustees.

The Function of a Foundation

T HE CONCEPT of the function of a foundation is closely interwoven with other threads in the pattern of philosophy and practice. In introducing a discussion of the problem of disentangling this skein, Keppel said:

> Please don't look for logical sequence in the discussion of foundation policies upon which I am about to embark. It isn't there. I've tried the different sections in half a dozen different orders without success. With so many different questions of principle arising in connection with the making of any particular grant, and so much to be said on both sides, I am consoling myself with the thought that perhaps the best way for you to grasp the many difficulties of the situation is precisely through the feeling of complexity and confusion which I am sure my treatment of the matter will furnish.[1]

Similarly, in his book covering the relationship of foundations to higher education, Hollis expressed the opinion that the principles and policies of the foundations are as complicated and involved as those that govern the institutions of higher learning in the United States.[2]

Historically, one of the chief concepts distinguishing the American foundation from its European counterpart is the

[1] Keppel, Frederick P., *The Foundation*, pp. 34–35.
[2] Hollis, Ernest V., *Philanthropic Foundations and Higher Education*, p. 27.

prevention of the ills of mankind rather than palliation. It is, of course, true that this concept was advanced in England at least as early as in the United States.[1] The absence of comparably large foundations in England, however, allowed no place for its practical application and refinement. In any event, the turn of the century saw the emergence of the large American foundation and a simultaneous enunciation of the principle of prevention. For instance, in 1906, one writer surmised:

> If I have rightly conceived the dominant idea of the modern philanthropy it is embodied in a determination to *seek out and to strike effectively at those organized forces of evil, at those particular causes of dependence and intolerable living conditions which are beyond the control of the individuals whom they injure and whom they too often destroy.*[2]

Commenting on philanthropy in general, John D. Rockefeller stated that it was hard to give away money successfully and that haphazard methods of giving it away were due to a lack of thought and effort. He pointed up these observations by alluding to the practice of giving to relieve present ills of mankind rather than attempting to eliminate or prevent the causes.[3]

It is not strange, then, that a few months after the first meeting of the Rockefeller Foundation a "memorandum on principles and policies" was adopted which embraced the following points:

1. Individual charity and relief were not to be considered.

2. Projects of a purely local character were to be excluded, unless they were in the nature of a demonstration.

3. No permanent good could be anticipated by giving aid for any purpose that was incapable of invoking a desire on the part of the recipient to assist and carry it forward.

4. Outside agencies should not become permanent or indefinite charges.

[1] Gray, B. Kirkman, *Philanthropy and the State*, or Social Politics, P. S. King and Co., London, 1908, p. 2; Hurlin, Ralph G., "Trends Shown in the Establishment of Recent Foundations," *Changing Conditions in Public Giving*, edited by Alfred Williams Anthony, p. 26.

[2] Devine, Edward T., "The Dominant Note of the Modern Philanthropy," *Proceedings of the National Conference of Charities and Correction*, 1906, p. 3.

[3] Allen, William H., *Modern Philanthropy*. Dodd, Mead and Co., New York, 1912, pp. 213–223.

5. Gifts in perpetuity to other institutions should not have tight restrictions.

6. Preventive projects were to be preferred to projects of a palliative type.[1]

Analysis of the foregoing principles reveals that, basically, they all relate to the principle of prevention rather than palliation. As they were applied another principle developed— concentration of effort.

Early reports of the Rockefeller Foundation and the Carnegie Corporation show an awareness and belief in this principle. Their income is cited as only a drop in the bucket compared to government or industrial budgets for parallel activities. Therefore, in order to exert any influence, they must concentrate their funds and avoid "scatteration giving." This accounts, in part, for a further principle of withdrawing from a project once its usefulness has been demonstrated. Despite this belief in the efficacy of concentration, however, it was felt that it should not be carried to the point that all projects calling for small budgets should be ignored or rejected. Rather, the question was one of emphasis.[2]

That all philanthropy was not following this trend of thought, however, is evidenced by the bitterness of an attack in 1921 on palliative giving. In an *Atlantic Monthly* article Cornelia J. Cannon held that to give aid of a temporary and palliative nature was a blunder. She admitted that some might suffer if such charity was curtailed, but maintained that in the long run more would benefit by its elimination. After all, she concluded, "Our task is not buttressing the weakness of our fellows with our strength, but organizing the energies of man to reconstruct his world."[3] A recent observer voiced somewhat the same conviction. He charged that "the shotgun method" became too prevalent in the operations of the Rockefeller Foundation after 1937. In addition to being a mistaken

[1] Fosdick, Raymond B., *The Story of the Rockefeller Foundation*, pp. 22–23.

[2] Carnegie Corporation of New York, *Annual Report*, 1927, p. 16; 1932, pp. 27–28. Rockefeller Foundation, *Annual Report*, 1917, pp. 19–21; 1924, pp. 9–11.

[3] Cannon, Cornelia J., "Philanthropic Doubts," *Atlantic Monthly*, vol. 128, September, 1921, p. 299.

principle, he continued, such practice made it impossible for anyone to gauge the relative effectiveness of programs.[1]

Implicit in these criticisms is the belief that "scatteration giving" or "the shotgun method" has a tendency toward palliation. In other words, many small projects cannot reach and remove the root causes of mankind's troubles.

What is the situation today? What do the foundations consider to be their function? The replies to the House Select Committee's Questionnaire throw some light on these questions. Section G-1 asks the direct question: "What, in your opinion, is the function of tax-exempt philanthropic and educational foundations in society today?"

Approximately one-fourth of the replies showed little awareness of the role they should be playing. Three foundations ignored the question completely. Five stated that they had neither the experience nor knowledge to answer the question and offered as reasons the limited purpose of their charters or self-imposed limitations of activity. Others answered in such vague and general terms as to make their replies relatively meaningless.

Another fourth of the answers were more specific. Several foundations expressed their concepts of function, however, only in terms of their own purpose or objective. One merely said that the function of a foundation was to carry out the will or intent of its founder. A few, construing the question very literally, concluded that there was no one function; that functions varied as much as the needs of the social order. The remainder of this group concerned themselves primarily with the socio-political implications of foundation functioning. Thus, they maintained that foundations relieved the taxpayer of some of his burdens. Conversely, they felt that foundations could be guided solely by impartial, nonpolitical motives, the end result being that the function of foundations was to serve as an alter ego to government or business, or to both. One foundation freely admitted that government could, of course, curtail or even abolish foundations,

[1] Flexner, Abraham, *Funds and Foundations*, pp. 83–88, 97–99.

. . . but something in the heart and soul of America would die if all endowed institutions were destroyed. The destruction of the foundation of general philanthropic purpose would almost certainly lead to attacks upon endowed educational and cultural institutions, and endowments for religious purposes would not be far behind.[1]

Venture Capital

Approximately half of the 54 foundations answering the Questionnaire stated, in one form or another, that the primary function of foundations is to provide the capital for worthwhile projects that cannot be financed from other sources. The phrase that these foundations employed in describing this concept is "venture" or "risk capital."

One foundation, in detailing its venture-capital concept, compared the function of the modern foundation to that of aiding pioneers in the early history of America. The frontier of knowledge, as was the old frontier, is difficult of access; therefore, funds are needed. Foundations, then, should provide the stakes for these treks into the unknown and unchartered wilderness of knowledge.[2]

Another foundation expressed the concept thus:

> The foundations act as catalysts in research and education through support of new ideas and invasion of unexplored fields of knowledge. Foundations can take gambles on new ideas which, until proven, need not be supported by universities or by public funds. By support of individuals and institutions foundations have been able to advance standards of education and research.[3]

In addition to the pioneering and gambling aspect, the neglected areas of man's activity were also pointed to as fertile fields for venture capital:

> There are also fields which, although not new or experimental, lack adequate support. The humanities are an outstanding example. Support from government and industry is forthcoming in

[1] Buhl Foundation, *Answers to Questionnaire*, p. 26.
[2] Carnegie Foundation for the Advancement of Teaching, *Answers*, p. 42.
[3] Josiah Macy, Jr., Foundation, *Answers*, p. 13.

large measure for the natural sciences, including biology and medicine, and the social sciences are receiving wide attention. Much less support is available for the humanities, which are as important as science to the health of a culture.[1]

The validity of the concept of venture capital was upheld by the Twentieth Century Fund. It reasoned that the function of philanthropy and education could be divided into two categories: (1) philanthropic and educational functions which communities have come to accept as necessary in the public administration of a modern state; (2) philanthropic and educational functions which communities consider desirable, but because of their nature not necessary or unsuited for state intervention. Examples in the first category are hospitals and universities. An example in the second category is religion. It is then pointed out that the public idea of what should be state or publicly supported has continually changed. Thus, in Galileo's Italy, state support of religion was practiced. Non-support of the experiments which he was conducting was also an accepted practice. In the United States today the practices are exactly reversed: private support for religion, public or state support for experimental work in the natural sciences. The conclusion, of course, is that foundations should provide the capital which programs that would advance man's knowledge lack for one reason or another.[2]

When did the venture-capital concept of function emerge? Hollis testified that "the theory of venture capital does not date back past World War I in foundation experience."[3] As a definitely enunciated principle this is probably true. In the earlier concept of prevention rather than palliation, however, it seems that the concept of venture capital is implicit. It would merely be a matter of time and experience until the latter would be clearly stated. Certainly by the 1920's several foundation officials were making conceptual statements that border very closely on that of venture capital. While head of the

[1] Old Dominion Foundation, *Answers*, p. 35.

[2] Twentieth Century Fund, *Answers*, pp. 42–44.

[3] *Hearings*, Statement of Ernest V. Hollis, p. 17.

Spelman Fund, Beardsley Ruml held that, in general, private funds were best used in projects of a novel or experimental nature or for those not yet accepted as a public responsibility.[1] George E. Vincent, while president of the Rockefeller Foundation, in a 1928 interview told a reporter that "foundations justify themselves in proportion as their trustees and officers recognize the duty not only to support tested projects but also to experiment, not blindly to follow tradition, to aim at quality not quantity of achievement, even to take certain risks for the sake of possible progress, not merely to play safe."[2]

The same feeling permeates the writings of Henry S. Pritchett, former president of the Carnegie Foundation for the Advancement of Teaching, and Frederick P. Keppel.

Testimony given before the House Select Committee in 1952 reveals a nearly unanimous verdict for the venture-capital concept.[3] One official stated that he had read previous testimony before appearing himself and noted this unanimity of opinion. He felt that he might be accused of plagiarism for echoing the same idea, but assured the Committee that this concept had been in his mind before he knew what others had testified.[4]

Many witnesses, espousing the concept of venture capital, were quick to point out the difficulties and disadvantages in applying the idea. One problem applies either to preventive efforts or the venture-capital concept—the need to act as an experimental standard-setting organization. The foundation should attempt to select projects which, once their value has been demonstrated, will find popular support. Thereupon, the foundation can disengage itself to sponsor new ventures. Otherwise, the venture-capital concept would die a-borning in con-

[1] Keppel, Frederick P., *The Foundation*, p. 43.

[2] Dodge, Faith Hunter, "In the Service of Humanity," *Pan-American Magazine*, vol. 41, December, 1928, p. 204.

[3] For examples see *Hearings*, Statement of F. Emerson Andrews, p. 44; James S. Simmons, pp. 86–87; Marshall Field, p. 449; Alfred P. Sloan, Jr., p. 454. For a somewhat dissenting opinion see *Hearings*, Statement of Alfred M. Kohlberg, pp. 669–671. Mr. Kohlberg objected to the use of foundation funds as venture capital in the field of "governmental policy."

[4] *Hearings*, Statement of Joseph E. Johnson, p. 583.

tinuing support of projects probably becoming less and less venturesome.[1] An example of the disadvantage of this withdrawal policy was offered by the president of the University of Missouri, who, in speaking of the interrelation of foundations and higher education, said that grants growing out of the venture-capital concept were apt to be "inciting" or "accelerating" grants and when a foundation withdrew from a project the institution sponsoring it was often at a loss for means to continue it, no matter how worth while or successful it might be. President Middlebush's conclusion was that it behooved institutional administrators to consider this disadvantage when initiating projects requiring foundation support and, conversely, if foundations initiated the project, they should adopt a more responsible and far-sighted attitude.[2]

Another difficulty voiced by many witnesses was one that seems inherent in the concept of venture capital. It is criticism on the part of a few or many of projects undertaken. Some felt that this criticism may have become more vocal because of the changing nature of the particular areas of foundation interest. In the late twenties and early thirties as the federal government and other public sources began to support health, agriculture, and the natural sciences to a greater and greater degree, foundations began to move into the social and humanistic areas where it was felt their limited funds could be utilized to the best advantage. It was clearly recognized that they were entering more controversial fields but the need was held to be so great and the potential rewards for mankind so enormous that they went ahead.[3] One witness explained, "When you turn to that field [humanistic and social studies], at every step you are stepping on somebody's toes." He held, however, that it was the proper function for foundations to plow ahead anyway, since if they did not, nobody would. And "if the boundaries of knowledge are pushed back and back and back so that our ignorance of ourselves and our fellowman and of other

[1] *Ibid.*, Statement of F. Emerson Andrews, pp. 46–47; Keppel, Frederick P., *The Foundation*, pp. 43–44.

[2] *Hearings*, Statement of Frederick Middlebush, p. 111.

[3] *Ibid.*, Statement of William I. Myers, p. 135; Dean Rusk, pp. 487–488.

nations is steadily reduced, there is hope for mankind, and unless those boundaries are pushed back there is no hope."[1]

Ford Foundation officials explained in great detail that their basic reason for braving possible criticism was their adherence to the venture-capital concept of the function of foundations. Henry Ford II, chairman of its Board of Trustees, reasoned that foundations, being human institutions, were bound to make mistakes. He indicated that mistakes in programs dealing with humanistic and social problems might evoke quite a bit of criticism, but he concluded that "it is better to risk mistakes in enterprising efforts to help solve such important problems than to leave the problems unsolved."[2]

Robert M. Hutchins, one of the associate directors of the Ford Foundation, suggested that the only remedy for this problem of criticism was to get the people to understand that the proper function of a foundation is to take calculated risks in controversial areas, namely, areas where other institutions and agencies dare not or cannot go. In addition, he warned the foundations themselves not to become afraid of criticism. He held that the way to guard against this is to have a constant influx of new personnel.[3]

One official discounted fear of criticism and stated that while his foundation was concerned about public opinion, the probability of criticism, fair and honest or otherwise, did not greatly influence decisions. He explained that his fellow officers felt that such criticism could not "put us out of business." Furthermore, the Board of Trustees, made up of men serving without compensation, could not be accused of harboring timorous souls. Thus, he said that he could not recall a single instance where fear of criticism had influenced a board decision.[4]

Actual implementation of the concept of venture capital was explained by this same witness at the Select Committee Hearings. He testified that capital was not ventured on experimental

---

[1] *Ibid.*, Statement of Russell C. Leffingwell, pp. 375–376.

[2] *Ibid.*, Statement of Henry Ford II, p. 220. See also statement of Paul G. Hoffman, pp. 229, 255.

[3] *Ibid.*, Statement of Robert M. Hutchins, pp. 282–284.

[4] *Ibid.*, Statement of Charles Dollard, pp. 339–340.

or risk projects merely because they were risky. Rather, a careful selection was made to find those which, although risky, gave most promise of proving truly effective in furthering the well-being of mankind. Phrases that were voiced in this connection were "pivotal points" and "looking for leverage." In other words, it was explained, "We are always looking for the place where you will get the maximum impact with a given amount of money."[1]

Two concrete examples of the application of the venture-capital concept were offered. One of these was the use of foundation funds for fellowships and other aids to young men of talent. It was pointed out, however, that this was not so easy as it might appear because identifying brains at an early age was a complex problem and that, even with the exercise of the possible judgment, a considerable degree of risk would be best taken since only a fair number of the persons selected would realize the estimates placed on their abilities.[2] The second example offered was support of basic research, particularly at the university level. Here, it was maintained, the inquiring mind should be provided the wherewithal, even though no practical application of the results of that inquiry might be immediately visible.[3]

Programs—Development

What is the basis of selection of the programs foundations institute? How do they differ in their approach to the problem of programming and planning? Or do some of them consider it a problem? Have there been any significant changes in this respect? Finally, in a general way, what has been the impact of the concepts of prevention and venture capital upon foundation programs? With the total number of grants, in the case of one foundation at least, running as high as one thousand annually,[4] one may well ponder the preceding questions.

[1] *Ibid.*, pp. 341–342.

[2] *Ibid.*, Statement of Dean Rusk, p. 491.

[3] *Ibid.*, Statement of Frederick Middlebush, p. 115; Alfred P. Sloan, Jr., p. 457; Dean Rusk, pp. 491–492.

[4] *Ibid.*, Statement of Dean Rusk, p. 479.

Those foundations giving great thought to ascertaining their function in our society, have also put great thought and effort into their programs. The reverse is also true. Thus, certain general, rational principles of programming tend to develop among those foundations that have given careful thought to their function. It may be noted, too, that those same foundations, with few exceptions, embrace the preventive venture-capital concept of function. The others present a hodgepodge of indiscriminancy, probably traceable to inertia; or they present programs that have been so finely delineated by donor or trustee action that there is little opportunity for alternative courses of action. In developing the history of programming, one is compelled to rely on the first group because the latter simply does not offer any explanation for the way in which its members do business.

The first annual report of the Rockefeller Foundation states that its early meetings were devoted to discussion as to what the best program might be for the new organization.[1] Keppel believed that there was a growing tendency for trustees to spend more time and thought in developing programs of action rather than in following the policy of drift and allowing applications for aid to indicate general lines of action. As proof of this contention he cited the shift from the habit of giving funds for general endowment purposes to support of institutions and activities whose work fitted into a specific foundation program. Thus, the Carnegie Corporation's grants for general endowment or equipment during the period 1921–1924 were shown as falling from 77 per cent of the total to 33 per cent.[2] Several foundation reports covering approximately the same period comment on this shift from gifts for general endowment to those for a specified purpose.[3] A fairly recent study of the type of gifts made to institutions of higher learning in the two decades following World War I provides substantial, statistical proof of this shift from gifts for endowment or general purposes

[1] Rockefeller Foundation, *Annual Report*, 1913–1914, p. 11.

[2] Keppel, Frederick P., *The Foundation*, pp. 40–42.

[3] General Education Board, *Annual Report*, 1929–1930, p. 3; Milbank Memorial Fund, *Twenty-Fifth Anniversary*, 1930, p. 37.

to those of a more specific nature. At the beginning of the period, four-fifths of the gifts were primarily for general endowment; by 1940 this had declined to 36.3 per cent of the total.[1]

This trend in programs, arising as it does primarily from a more positive approach on the part of foundations, should not be construed as an indication that programs are formed in ivory towers. Quite the contrary is true. Consultation and studies outside the foundations have increasingly been an integral part of foundation programming.

Consultation, however, is not practiced by all the foundations. A 1936 study of 55 foundations showed that over half made no use at all of outside consultation.[2] In 1938 Hollis drew somewhat the same conclusions.[3] This might lead one to suspect that those foundations not consulting outside sources would do the greatest amount of program planning inside. The exact reverse is true. Reason for this statement lies in a comparison of the answers to two questions asked by the 1952 Select Committee Questionnaire. One of these, number 7 of Section B, asked: "Is any individual or group of individuals charged with the duty of originating and developing plans, programs, and proposals for the distribution of your funds?"

The other question, number 6 of Section C, asked: "In the making of gifts, grants, loans, contributions, or other expenditures does your organization consult with any other organizations such as the United States Government, educational groups, religious groups, labor groups, veterans' societies, patriotic societies, foreign governments, other foreign agencies? If so, explain."

Of the 54 foundations answering the first question, B-7, 19 indicated that no specific individuals in the foundation were directly charged with a planning or programming responsibility. All except three of this same 19, in answering the sec-

[1] Goldthorpe, J. Harold, *Higher Education, Philanthropy, and Federal Tax Exemption*, edited by Dorothy Leemon. Series V, no. 7, American Council on Education Studies. The Council, Washington, 1944, pp. 7–8.

[2] Coffman, Harold C., *American Foundations*, p. 32.

[3] Hollis, Ernest V., *Philanthropic Foundations and Higher Education*, p. 107.

ond question, C-6, indicated that they consulted no outside sources in the making of gifts or grants.

It is admitted that the two questions bear on somewhat dissimilar phases of foundation activity. Too, the negative answers to the first question do not preclude the possibility that planning of programs, perhaps a great deal of it, is accomplished in those organizations. At the very least, however, the conclusion seems inescapable that there is a definite correlation between evidence of thoughtful program planning and outside consultation.

What are the approaches used by foundations that consult outside sources? First and obviously, there is the simple process of the foundation official getting the opinion of a man from outside the foundation on a proposed program. As the foundations grow in experience, we witness the growing practice of dependence on recognized groups of experts rather than individuals. Indeed, several foundation historians attribute, at least partially, the creation of such organizations as the Social Science Research Council and the American Council of Learned Societies to a response to foundation need for groups of experts who could aid them in planning and programming and, later, in implementing the projects chosen.[1]

A third method used in developing programs is the study of the principles and practices of other foundations. Various reports of the Carnegie Corporation of New York, in urging the preservation of foundation records, stressed their importance as guides to both new and old foundations.[2] It is hard to gauge the extent of the use of this method; however, several foundations have asserted that at the time they became active they took advantage of such records. The Rosenwald Fund, for instance, when it really began operation as a foundation in 1928, made a careful study of the programs of older foundations to find a program that was not duplicated by foundations or other

[1] Keppel, Frederick P., *The Foundation*, pp. 69–74; Hollis, Ernest V., *Philanthropic Foundations and Higher Education*, pp. 109–110. See also Carnegie Corporation of New York, *Annual Report*, 1936, p. 39.
[2] Carnegie Corporation of New York, *Annual Report*, 1930, pp. 11–12; 1941, pp. 50–51.

agencies.[1] The Falk Foundation stated in its organizational report:

> It was obvious that the Board's first task was to learn what was most worth giving to, and what methods of giving might best accomplish a constructive and lasting good. Accordingly, it was determined that action on applications should be held in abeyance until the Executive Director of the Foundation had made a thorough study of first, the programs and policies of older foundations; and second, such neglected fields for giving as might be discovered in his survey of the programs of the trusts.[2]

The Twentieth Century Fund asserts that it, too, considered the activities of the older foundations in developing its program.[3]

Another method used is the study, conducted by persons inside or outside the foundations and usually devoted to the consideration of a limited portion of the proposed program. This method was particularly useful to the Rockefeller Foundation, the Carnegie Corporation of New York, and the General Education Board in the formation of their programs in higher education. Many of the studies, because of various factors, were confidential in their nature; consequently, it is difficult to determine their relative influence in programming.[4] Published reports, such as that made by Abraham Flexner on medical education,[5] however, indicate that they have probably had a very great influence.

An interesting and novel variant on this method is the approach used by the recently reorganized Ford Foundation. It merits elaboration. Rather than trying to find areas or fields neglected by others in which to labor, the leaders of this Foundation felt that they should attempt to find out directly from the people all over the country the consensus as to how the

[1] Embree, Edwin R., and Julia Waxman, *Investment in People*, pp. 32–33.

[2] Maurice and Laura Falk Foundation, *Report*, 1930–1932, p. 2.

[3] Twentieth Century Fund, *Annual Report*, 1933, pp. 8–9.

[4] Hollis, Ernest V., *Philanthropic Foundations and Higher Education*, pp. 28–29.

[5] Flexner, Abraham, *Medical Education in the United States and Canada:* A Report to the Carnegie Foundation for the Advancement of Teaching. Bulletin 4. The Foundation, New York, 1910.

Ford Foundation should use its resources. The chairman of the Study Group, H. Rowan Gaither, Jr., thereupon organized a committee which "in the course of a few months . . . covered a quarter of a million miles by air travel, and put in about $7\frac{1}{2}$ man-years, not counting the time of the interviewees and conferees; they directly conferred with over a thousand men and women in the United States." This committee determined the Foundation's program, not by seeking and studying fields in which to labor, such as medicine, education, and so on, but rather by looking for the most pressing problems confronting mankind all over the world. It was primarily on the basis of this peripatetic analysis of problem areas that the global program of the Ford Foundation was formulated.[1]

The foundations that give continuous thought to planning their programs have always tried to keep abreast of changing conditions. The periods immediately following the two world wars have apparently been periods of the greatest transition. This is only natural, for the whole structure of world society underwent changes as a result of these cataclysms. In general, foundation programs have changed in the following manner. After World War I they shifted from programs of giving for general purposes to specific programs with particular emphasis on research and study in the troublesome and relatively neglected fields of human experience. Since World War II more and more programs have attempted to remedy the problems in these fields by education, demonstration, and so forth.

Today, approximately two-thirds of the larger foundations mentioned previously as answering the 1952 Questionnaire seem very eager to keep their programs up to date. These foundations indicated that they considered the planning of programs a very important portion of administration. Quite a few stated that programming was primarily performed by the trustees. Most of them, however, allocate program development to the chief executive officer, a staff member, or a combination of both. This latter practice appears to be the policy

[1] *Hearings*, Statement of H. Rowan Gaither, Jr., pp. 195–218. See also *Ibid.*, Statement of Paul G. Hoffman, p. 255; *Report of the Study for the Ford Foundation on Policy and Program*, 1949, pp. 9–25.

of those foundations with relatively larger resources, operating in a variety of fields. Only one instance was found where the programming function was delegated to a group outside the foundation.

Hand in hand with programming is the continuation of the consulting policy by this same group of foundations. Both individuals and groups are consulted. It can be noted that consultation with the various organs of the federal government appears to be an increasingly common practice, particularly in the fields of education and social welfare at home, and in all phases of foundation activity abroad. Various societies heretofore mentioned, such as the Social Science Research Council and the American Council of Learned Societies, are also frequently consulted.[1]

Program and the Venture-Capital Function

The prevention and venture-capital function is abundantly illustrated by past foundation programs in the natural sciences, medicine, and agriculture. Witness the Rockefeller Foundation's hookworm, malaria, and yellow fever campaigns, and the Carnegie Corporation of New York's aid in financing the Flexner Report. Very recently, of course, we have the ventures taken by the Rockefeller Foundation in advancing funds for the construction of a cyclotron at the University of California; research made possible by this instrument had much to do with the creation of the atomic bomb. Such foundation ventures, however, are now taken for granted; their initial experimental nature has been forgotten in the face of the indisputable results, and they are now almost universally applauded.

Quite the contrary has been true in the field of education (used in the broad sense) and especially in the humanities and social sciences. As Keppel explained, the average American regards the natural sciences, the humanities, and the social sciences in three different ways. The first he trusts; he does not understand them or even pretend to, but he trusts them, for

---

[1] *Questionnaire*, sec. B-7, 8; sec. C-6. See pp. 129, 130.

they have given him material comforts and stirred his imagination. The second he does not even think about, except possibly when news of the opening of some Egyptian tomb is published. The third make him uncomfortable and "in no mood to contribute toward their solution [that is, problems in the social sciences] by supporting the very steps he extols when they are applied to problems in the natural sciences." Thus, Keppel concluded that the natural sciences will receive ever-increasing public support; the humanities will slowly get a little more; but the social sciences will continue to depend on the foundations for their support for an indefinite period.[1] It is in these latter two fields, which comprise a majority of the subjects compounded in that vague term, general or liberal education, that the sharpest and clearest illustrations of programs resulting from the preventive venture-capital concept are to be found. Therefore, this section will primarily be devoted to foundation programs in liberal or general education.

The first thing to be noted in connection with foundation programs in education is that probably they have constituted the largest percentage of total programs. A half-dozen authorities, ranging over a period of sixteen years, attest this fact.[2] A survey of the 54 foundations answering the 1952 Questionnaire reveals essentially the same situation. Virtually all of them, in one way or another, listed education as a part of their programs.[3]

Lindeman believed that all donors had education in mind when they made their bequests.[4] This interest in education extends from the creators of many of the large foundations right down to present-day donors and officials. The chairman of the board of one of the largest, for instance, testified recently

[1] Keppel, Frederick P., *Philanthropy and Learning*, pp. 25–29.

[2] Lindeman, Eduard C., *Wealth and Culture*, pp. 20–27; Embree, Edwin R., "The Business of Giving Away Money," *Harper's Magazine*, vol. 161, August, 1930, p. 328; Hollis, Ernest V., *Philanthropic Foundations and Higher Education*, pp. 121–126; Seybold, Geneva, compiler, *American Foundations and Their Fields*, 4th ed., Raymond Rich Associates, New York, 1939, p. 35; Harrison, Shelby M., and F. Emerson Andrews, *American Foundations for Social Welfare*, pp. 79–81.

[3] *Questionnaire*, sec. E-3a. See p. 133.

[4] Lindeman, Eduard C., *Wealth and Culture*, p. 25.

that "the enterprise of education is perhaps the most important single enterprise that there is in the United States of America."[1]

What are the reasons for this deep and continuing interest?

Lindeman believed that donor interest and foundation aid reflect the American belief that the way to "get ahead" socially and economically is through education.[2]

This assumption, based as it is on economic determinism, contains an element of truth, but it overlooks the idealistic and spiritual beliefs that form so large a part of the American motivational pattern. This writer believes that the continuing interest in education reflects the basic American philosophy of progress. Despite the many present-day Spenglerians foretelling doom, Americans generally have an implicit faith that by study and learning the world will become a better and better place in which to live. Both the men who founded and those who have guided the foundations shared this belief. Tying in this belief with the concept of prevention rather than palliation, it is readily understandable why so many foundations sponsor educational programs. For by study and learning many of the woes of mankind could be alleviated or eliminated right at the source, the mind of man itself. Now, education is composed of two processes. First, there is the transmittal of culture from one generation to the next. Second, there is the creation, or derivation, or alchemizing, or call it what you will, of new knowledge; in other words, the taking of what is acquired under the first process and producing, by various means and methods, something that was not there before. This second process is, or should be, the function of higher education.

In general, foundations operating on the preventive venture-capital concept of function have been primarily concerned with the second or creative aspect of education and a large portion of their educational programs has been devoted to higher education. They have aided the first when the base or method for transmission of culture has either been absent or impaired. This, in a general way, seems to explain the origin

[1] *Hearings*, Statement of Russell C. Leffingwell, p. 372.
[2] Lindeman, Eduard C., *Wealth and Culture*, p. 26.

and changes in the educational programs of the foundations embracing the preventive venture-capital concept.

It explains, for instance, the pension program of the Carnegie Foundation for the Advancement of Teaching, which, while it provided pensions for teachers, did far more. It provided a sound base for secondary and higher education in the United States, both faculty- and curricula-wise.

It explains the activities of the General Education Board to provide a base for secondary and higher education in the South which, owing to the ravishing effects of the Civil War, was gravely impaired.

It explains the broad shifts in educational programs which took place in the last half-century. Thus, the period from 1900 until World War I saw foundation attention focused mainly on the base or transmissional aspects of education in the form of gifts for endowment and buildings. The period from the end of World War I to 1924–1925 saw programs entailing grants for special endowments, such as medical buildings, equipment, and so forth. Since that time, with the increasing public support of the first phase of education, the foundations have displayed increasing interest in the second. Research programs, for example, have been increasingly aided. Keppel, in 1930, said: "The prosecution of fundamental researches will remain one of the major opportunities, perhaps the major opportunity, of the foundations, so long as they themselves endure."[1] Various foundation records, and the writings of persons connected with foundations, indicate the same belief.[2]

Some light is thrown on the relationship between the preventive venture-capital concept and education by the answers to the 1952 House Select Committee Questionnaire. Generally speaking, foundations that embrace the preventive venture-capital concept of function are those that have taken the lead

[1] Keppel, Frederick P., The Foundation, pp. 89–90.

[2] General Education Board, Annual Report, 1927–1928, p. 5; John and Mary R. Markle Foundation, Annual Report, 1936, p. 5; Rockefeller Foundation, Annual Report, 1929, p. 175; Fosdick, Raymond B., The Story of the Rockefeller Foundation, pp. 140–142; Hollis, Ernest V., Philanthropic Foundations and Higher Education p. 298.

in developing programs devoted to the second or creative phase of education. The others devote their funds primarily to providing buildings, general endowment, and so forth. Too, this latter group tends to operate on a restricted, local basis rather than a national or international one.

The same pattern regarding consultation, discussed in a general way in the preceding section, is apparent here. Foundation programs in education founded on the preventive venture-capital concept do the greatest amount of outside consultation. The others do relatively little or none at all.

None of the foundations makes attempts, per se, to present divergent views on controversial educational issues. Their position seems well taken. It would be asking too much of a group at all convinced of the value of a specific educational program to support one that is exactly contrary.

All the foundations, many of them probably not aware of philanthropic history, either make no grants to religious groups at all or, if so, they do not allow the religious factor to be a consideration when designing their educational program.[1]

One, if not the most persistent, question concerning the educational foundation that has cropped up pertains almost solely to foundations that embrace the preventive venture-capital concept of function. This question involves the degree of control exercised by the foundations over the educational system in the United States. Although the broader aspects of this question will be considered in the next chapter, it is so intimately associated with education that it cannot be ignored here.

Are the foundations in large measure controlling our educational system through the application of the preventive venture-capital concept? The contention of some is that gifts for endowments or buildings can, at the most, be only limited-control factors, whereas grants for research and specific programs can guide and shape the drift of ideas. Thus, harried administrators, in quest of financial assistance, would tend to adapt their faculty policy and curricula to the established policy of the particular foundation.

[1] *Questionnaire*, sec. E-3a–h. See p. 133.

Perhaps the best way to answer this question is not to turn to the denials of foundation officials or educators, but to discuss briefly an educational program which in the past received some foundation support. Variously termed, it is commonly known as "progressive education." One of its generally accepted doctrines is that methodology in teaching is as, if not more, important than knowledge of the subject taught. Thus, it seemed to make little difference if the teacher really knew a particular subject. Of major importance was his ability to teach it. The classic example of the result of this concept is the student matriculating in one of the great midwestern universities who failed mathematics but received the grade of 100 in how to teach it.[1]

A development in this movement was the proliferation of courses dealing with methodology to the point that substantive courses were being crowded out of the curriculum. And even if the curriculum did include an adequate number, students frequently found it possible to elect relatively few, since the number of methodological courses for the fulfillment of degree and teacher certificate requirements was prescribed. The net result of the system was that it produced many individuals knowing the methods exactly but having nothing to teach.

In supporting some projects in progressive education, the foundations from time to time have been labeled inaugurators or backers of the idea as a whole. Yet, today, two of the outstanding educators of the country, who were very closely associated with either a university or foundation while foundation support of progressive education was being provided, have openly expressed their opposition to many of the ideas associated with progressive education. Indeed, one of them is now an associate director of the Ford Foundation, which is providing money for The Fund for the Advancement of Education. This Fund, in turn, has inaugurated the so-called "Arkansas Experiment," which runs contrary to progressive education's emphasis on methodology.[2]

[1] *Hearings*, Statement of Henry M. Wriston, p. 185.

[2] *Ibid.*, pp. 184–190; Robert M. Hutchins, pp. 267–279. See also *Ibid.*, Statement of Alvin C. Eurich, pp. 310–315.

Even if the foundations wished to control or direct education, it would be a very difficult thing for them to do. It has
been aptly said, "A professor is a man who thinks otherwise."
Probably, foundation support was given, for a time, to progressive education because it was a "new" idea or approach that
might offer a solution to various pressing educational needs.

What seems a most fitting answer to this question of influence or control was that given at the recent Hearings of the
House Select Committee by one of the educators referred to
above. When questioned as to the extent "educators and the
educational institutions lead the foundations, or in reverse, the
extent to which the foundations tend to lead the educators and
educational institutions,"[1] he replied, "I think it is a mutual
influence."[2]

[1] *Ibid.*, Statement of Harold M. Keele, p. 176.
[2] *Ibid.*, Statement of Henry M. Wriston, p. 176.

Freedom of Action

WORDSWORTH's immortal words concerning Englishmen can also be applied to foundations; they "must be free or die." This is especially true if they are to carry out the preventive venture-capital concept of function, to which a majority of the larger ones adhere. In examining the statutes relating to foundations we find that American jurisprudence has traditionally recognized this fact by not hindering their growth with crippling legislation.

Legal Aspects

It has already been noted that foundations are allowed a wide latitude in the manner and means by which they are created. In large part this develops from the dual system of government set up by a constitution which reflected distrust of centralization of power. Thus, foundations can be established by a variety of means under the aegis of the federal or a state government. Also, the widest possible freedom is allowed a donor in selecting his philanthropy. Section 101 (6) of the Internal Revenue Code, under which the vast majority of the larger foundations function, provides tax exemption in the following terms:

> Corporations, and any community chest, fund, or foundation, organized and operated exclusively for religious, charitable, scientific, literary or educational purposes, or for the prevention

of cruelty to children or animals, no part of the net earnings of which inures to the benefit of any private shareholder or individual, and no substantial part of the activities of which is carrying on propaganda, or otherwise attempting, to influence legislation.

Thus, very general statements of purpose such as "the welfare of mankind" have been interpreted as socially useful, and deserving of tax exemption.

Once they are created, what amount of freedom are foundations afforded?

Supervision over charitable trusts and foundations is primarily a state function. Federal jurisdiction is limited to the usual appellate powers of the courts and application of the taxing powers.[1] Basically, both state and federal supervision rest on a combination of chartering and taxing powers.

Machinery for the supervision of charitable trusts and foundations by the states is provided by the court. However, the court does not raise issues concerning foundations; it only hears them. Another state official, usually the attorney general, is the one who actually investigates and initiates any action that might bring a foundation into a court of law. The means whereby the attorney general keeps himself informed, and thus supervises foundation activities is usually the periodic report of the foundation. But in most states, the system of reporting is in a chaotic condition. Even in the few states where there is machinery for enforcing reporting, the problem of setting it in motion still remains, and is usually complicated by inadequate staffing in the attorney general's office. In the last analysis, then, reporting is usually dependent upon the cooperation of the various trustees.

Because of the tax exemption granted foundations and charitable trusts recently there has been a tendency in two or three states for tax boards and commissions to exercise control indirectly over such institutions by denying or removing tax exemption.

---

[1] Except for controls over federal corporations.

Federal supervision over charitable trusts and foundations rests squarely on the federal government's ability to grant and revoke tax exemption to those organizations. Issuance and revocation of such exemption chiefly depends, as is the case with the states, on written reports furnished by the foundation. The Bureau of Internal Revenue has the most direct responsibility for supervision of philanthropic organizations, since these reports are forwarded to the Bureau and processed, ruled on, and filed there. The degree of supervision is, again as in the case of the states, subject to manpower limitations. In contrast to the state governments, however, the Bureau of Internal Revenue performs the role of court, attorney general, and tax commission, all in one. Appeal from decisions, of course, can be taken to the federal courts.[1]

In the case of both state and federal governments illegal operation may lead to revocation of tax exemption, or possible prosecution for fraud. Recent testimony by a Bureau of Internal Revenue official shows, however, that these prosecutions are reserved for only the most flagrant cases and are few in number.[2] Once a foundation has been established there is very little supervision of its activities. To quote one commentary: "The freedom of charitable foundations to operate as they please is virtually complete."[3]

Within such limitations, then, the donor has complete freedom in defining the purpose of his philanthropy and the manner in which he sets it up. His foundation, once set up, has complete freedom in planning its program. Nowhere do we find the omniscient group—lay, religious, educational, or governmental—spelling out in exact and precise terms how philanthropic funds shall be expended. *Here, in this writer's estimation, lies the key to the rise, rapid growth, and influence of American foundations. It is the opportunity to do good unhampered by confusing bureau-*

[1] The basis for the foregoing interpretation is Eleanor K. Taylor's *Public Accountability of Foundations and Charitable Trusts*. Russell Sage Foundation, New York, 1953.

[2] *Hearings*, Statement of Norman A. Sugarman, pp. 79–80.

[3] "The Modern Philanthropic Foundation: A Critique and a Proposal," *Yale Law Journal*, vol. 59, February, 1950, p. 484.

cratic restrictions. Foundations are the natural outgrowth and expression of the private enterprise system. The essential ingredient in both can be called "freedom of action."

Foreign Activity

Have the larger foundations and charitable trusts of the United States fully utilized their unique freedom of action? The answer is an emphatic "yes." The widest range and multiplicity of programs has been inaugurated under this principle. Perhaps the epitome in its application and development is the foreign activity engaged in by many of the larger foundations. Unless, of course, restricted by charter, the foundations are perfectly free to carry on their activities anywhere in the world, foreign governments permitting.

Of the 54 foundations responding to the House Select Committee Questionnaire, approximately one-fourth indicated that their programs included at that time or had previously included some foreign projects.[1] Without exception those in this grouping embrace the preventive venture-capital concept. Prominent among their number are the three largest: Ford Foundation, Rockefeller Foundation, and Carnegie Corporation of New York.

Six of these maintain offices and staffs in foreign countries. They tend, however, to locate in different countries. Thus, one foundation has an office in France, another in Mexico, another in India. This lack of duplication is not due to prior consultation but primarily to varying interests at different periods on the part of the individual foundations.

Accustomed as we have grown to sizable United States government bureaucracies abroad, the foreign staff employed by these foundations is amazingly small. The number ranges from several informal representatives of the John Simon Guggenheim Memorial Foundation, who never receive more than $50 a year for expenses, to the 46 full-time staff members employed by the Rockefeller Foundation in its various foreign offices. Because of its historical interest in international medicine and

[1] *Questionnaire*, sec. E-3, 4; sec. F-1. See pp. 133–134.

health the latter employs the largest staff. The average number of employees abroad is five or six persons per foundation.

During the past five years, the proportion of the total amount expended abroad by these foundations to that expended in the United States averaged 10 per cent. Highest, again, was the Rockefeller Foundation, which averaged approximately 25 per cent for the period.

One is struck very forcefully by the policy either stated or implied in the foreign activities of these foundations. It is the clearest distillation of the preventive venture-capital concept. This policy is one of preventing war, and, concomitantly, promoting peace.

In striving to promote international peace, the foundations have adopted various approaches. Exchange of persons, particularly scientists and scholars, has been one of the most favored devices. The Kellogg Foundation, in explaining its policy and working practices in this respect, stated:

> One of the major objectives of the Foundation's international programs has been to bring about better international understanding through cultural exchange. . . . Fellows are placed in the educational centers best suited to prepare them for their work after they return home. In planning programs attention is given to the social and cultural as well as professional needs of fellows and they are provided with an opportunity to become acquainted with United States cultural centers. They are visited at regular intervals by members of the Foundation staff and each fellow has a preceptor at the educational center to whom he may look for advice and counsel.[1]

Another method utilized has been the establishment of "area programs" at various universities in the United States and abroad for the intensive study of all aspects of the culture of a particular foreign area or country. Language, history, literature, and other such subjects form the curricula of such centers. Outstanding examples are the Russian Institute at Columbia University, and similar programs at Stanford University and the University of Washington. The Rockefeller Foundation

---

[1] Kellogg Foundation, *Answers to Questionnaire*, pp. 61–64.

and the Carnegie Corporation of New York have been largely responsible for promoting this work. Various other methods that aim at enlarging knowledge about our relations with foreign countries have also been employed. Chief among these are study and discussion groups and aid for scholarly studies in various fields of international relations. Projects of this nature have been instituted at home and abroad.

The Carnegie Endowment for International Peace is the only one of this group engaged in international activities that was chartered solely for work toward international peace.[1] The expenditures of the Ford Foundation, however, for the promotion of peace probably exceed those of the Endowment. One-fifth of the Ford Foundation's total effort is specifically devoted to programs in this area. It may be noted here that this Foundation has instituted projects which include all the peace promotional types heretofore mentioned.

None of the larger foundations operating in foreign areas has attempted to prescribe what percentage of its funds should be spent abroad. The foundations apparently feel that the prime consideration is the goal. Thus, in answering questions raised at the Hearings before the House Select Committee of 1952 as to the wisdom of granting tax exemption for foundation expenditures in foreign fields, Paul Hoffman expressed the opinion that all foreign activity and expenditures should be related to the goal of peace; that being the foundation goal, it made no difference whether the money was spent at home or abroad. He concluded that, in the last analysis, every dollar spent abroad might repay the American people many times over if permanent peace were obtained.[2]

Foundations carrying on foreign activities also engage in extensive consultation regarding their projects. As might be expected, the United States Department of State is the organization most frequently consulted. United Nations is also frequently consulted. Advice is usually asked, too, of a variety of other organizations, both at home and abroad, particularly

---

[1] *Hearings*, Statement of Joseph E. Johnson, p. 581.
[2] *Ibid.*, Statement of Paul G. Hoffman, pp. 232–237.

when a specific project is in the planning stage. The Ford Foundation reply to the question of consultation may be considered typical:

> Policies and programs dealing with international relations are developed only after fullest consultation with individuals and groups not employed or otherwise directly connected with the Foundation. These include men in Government informed on the particular questions involved, and men who are interviewed in on-the-ground investigations abroad. Other points of consultation are the many voluntary American associations with long experience abroad. . . . The agencies and individuals consulted cannot be neatly catalogued; they have varied with the country and the nature of the project.

The Foundation then added that in individual countries the heads of government, leaders in ministries affected, and United States diplomatic and technical staff were normally consulted, but that in some areas consultation with foreign governments was limited because of unstable economic and political conditions.[1]

This policy of consultation, however, is not to be construed as an abridgment of the principle of freedom of action. In their relationship with the United Nations, for instance, all the foundations that engaged in foreign activities stated that they had no official ties with that agency. In their relations with our Department of State they have kept the Department informed of their activities and have been friendly, but independent. Various officers of these foundations have served the State Department as consultants or in other part-time capacities. Too, many of their projects were inaugurated almost as dual ventures. But foundation projects have not been controlled by the views of the State Department nor have their agreements with foreign countries been subject to State Department approval.[2]

In contacts with foreigners and their institutions and governments, the foundations have also guarded their freedom of

---

[1] Ford Foundation, *Answers to Questionnaire*, pp. 49–51.

[2] *Questionnaire*, sec. E-3b, 4a–h; sec. F-1–8; see pp. 133, 134, 135–136. See also *Hearings*, Statement of Paul G. Hoffman, pp. 233–234.

action. In most instances, therefore, the foundations do not operate directly unless they have the very fullest cooperation and understanding with the host country. Very often such understandings are spelled out in written agreements. The foundations, rather, tend to make grants to private organizations and individuals. In no case do these foundations deal with a particular political party or group in any foreign country. Nor do they allow any agents, employees, or affiliates to engage in political activity in any foreign country. The reasons are, of course, obvious. If these foundations were to engage in political activity of any kind, their freedom to operate in such countries would sooner or later be curtailed or abolished.

Independence of Grantees

The question of the degree of independence of grantees merits consideration at this point, for the independence of their grantees is a reciprocal principle of the foundation's own freedom of action. The one cannot be logically or even morally justified unless the other is also true.

The allegation that foundations are schemes to ensnare, trap, and control those who accept their largess has been one of the most consistent criticisms leveled at them. The very emergence of foundations occasioned such an outcry. For instance, one of the most outspoken critics of the Carnegie Foundation for the Advancement of Teaching and the General Education Board was Bishop Warren A. Candler of the Methodist Episcopal Church, South. In a booklet published in 1909 and significantly titled *Dangerous Donations and Degrading Doles,* or A Vast Scheme for Capturing and Controlling the Colleges and Universities of the Country, Candler maintained that universities were one of the most powerful units, if not the most powerful, in molding society. European experiences were cited as proof. He held that the foundations' offer to aid education was nothing but an attempt to seize thorough-going control of the country. Once such aid was accepted, he predicted a drive for federal aid to education and a movement to make the Commissioner of Education a Cabinet officer. From that, he contended, it would be only a short step to federal supervision of education. Next would come fixed and guided courses of study in all fields: economic, intellectual, moral, and social. With the last, he touched on the implications that such a "national" control of education might have for the racial situation in the South and California. He concluded that the various sections of the nation and particularly the South should reject the proffered aid of the foundations and should pay for and control their own educational systems.[1]

Somewhat later, from a different section of the country, a famous bacteriologist and professor at the Harvard Medical School voiced, although much less vehemently, several aspects of the same criticism. Zinsser, however, wanted foundation money but deplored "control" of the direction of medicine by some foundations. He favored foundations making grants for specified purposes but "leaving the details of procedure and organization entirely to the governing bodies of the beneficiary institutions," thus eliminating the "irritation and the apprehensions . . . from a relationship which should be one purely of gratitude for great benefactions."[2]

An address to the Medical Society of the County of New York in 1931 echoed Zinsser. While admitting that many foundations, particularly the Rockefeller and Carnegie groups, have accomplished notable work in medicine, the view was expressed that some of the others "must learn that their function is to provide means for the advancement of thought, not to control thought."[3]

In *Wealth and Culture* Lindeman dismissed influencing of grantees with an offhand, "Such influence is obvious. . . ."[4]

What does one of the most experienced of the foundation officials say about this matter? In the 1930's Keppel was not

[1] Candler, Warren A., *Dangerous Donations and Degrading Doles*, or A Vast Scheme for Capturing and Controlling the Colleges and Universities of the Country. Privately printed, Atlanta, Ga.(?), 1909.

[2] Zinsser, Hans, "The Perils of Magnanimity," *Atlantic Monthly*, vol. 139, February, 1927, p. 249.

[3] Kopetzky, Samuel J., *Foundations and Their Trends*. Privately printed, New York, 1931, p. 14.

[4] Lindeman, Eduard C., *Wealth and Culture*, p. 19.

sure of the foundation's tendency to take control over grantees. He admitted that the "bulk" of "recent criticism" had been directed at this aspect of foundation practice, but he maintained that it was a hard question to answer.[1]

In a subsequent foundation report Keppel stated:

> Relations between the foundations and what may be called the grant-consuming public have been steadily improving. It is no longer felt by applicants that obeisance need be made as a condition of receiving attention, for it is recognized that the foundation is quite as anxious to find outstanding opportunities for carrying out its trust as the applicant is eager to receive financial aid.[2]

Several years later, in speaking of trustees, he said:

> The most significant change of all is in their attitude toward the recipients of grants. They no longer feel, as they once did, that the act of paying the piper confers *ipso facto* the right to call the tune in all its notes and quavers.[3]

Apparently Keppel felt that relations in this delicate field left much to be desired in early foundation days. A more optimistic tone is shown later, however. Much of the credit for the improvement, granting it to be valid, must go to this foundation philosopher. His approach in this field throws light on how a meeting of minds can be arrived at without coercion.

> A foundation must not try either to be too efficient itself or to enforce too much efficiency upon others. In the preliminary stages of reaching an understanding, the tempers of its officers may be tried by badly organized meetings and conferences and by discursive presentations, but with patience a meeting of minds can ultimately be achieved. Any attempt to help in the administration of grants after they have been voted tends to break down the recipient's sense of full responsibility.[4]

This question of the relative independence of grantees springs in a measure from the follow-up procedures inaugu-

---

[1] Keppel, Frederick P., *The Foundation*, pp. 47–48.
[2] Carnegie Corporation of New York, *Annual Report*, 1931, p. 29.
[3] *Ibid.*, 1938, p. 47.
[4] *Ibid.*, 1941, p. 50.

rated by a vast majority of the larger foundations. These developed out of a desire to see that their money was not being wasted, and to compile a historical record that might prove useful in guiding future policy.[1]

The answers of 54 foundations to the House Select Committee throw some light on the question.[2] Eight of them employed little or no follow-up procedure. Some were of the operating type; therefore the question did not concern them. One gave as its reason for not following up grants that it had "complete confidence" in its grantees. The others stated that their grants were for definite and specific purposes and the results were apparent with little or no investigating.

Over half of the 54 followed up their grants on a very informal basis. Their chief reliance was on written progress reports from the grantees. For example, one foundation answered:

> No formal "follow-up" is made. In our letter of notification to the grantee we request copies of the published reports of scientific work resulting from our grants. These, together with progress reports, are in our files.[3]

Some 10 or 15 foundations had adopted formal procedures in following up grants. They explained that thorough investigations preceded each grant. Once the grant was made, the follow-up procedures normally took one of three forms or a combination of all three. (1) Officers and staff members spent a substantial portion of their time visiting grantee institutions or individuals. It was pointed out that training and experience taught these officials to gauge progress, but not to attempt to direct or control. (2) Routine progress reports, or, in some cases, mere summaries when the work was completed. (3) Budgetary reports; apparently great emphasis is placed on this portion of the follow-up. It was explained that this procedure was not very necessary on grants given in a lump sum. On

---

[1] Keppel, Frederick P., *The Foundation*, pp. 68–69.
[2] *Questionnaire*, sec. C-3. See p. 130.
[3] Josiah Macy, Jr., Foundation, *Answers to Questionnaire*, p. 8.

those calling for renewal or spaced over a period of years,
however, such reports assured the foundations that no frauds
were being perpetrated by their grantees. If such a situation
were exposed, remedial action could be taken before further
installments on such long-term appropriations were paid. It
was added that the actual application of these three procedures
varied in accordance with the nature of the grantee: an institution would be handled differently from an individual; a
large grant, differently from a small one, and so on.

Inevitably, of course, the thin line between the natural concern that money be well spent and outright control or direction
has probably been crossed on occasion. One expert witness
before the House Select Committee, for instance, acknowl-
edged that there was this very fine line between following up
grants for efficiency's sake, and encroachment on the independence of grantees. He and succeeding witnesses, however,
felt that the foundations had exercised a considerable degree of
restraint and had very carefully differentiated between control
and counsel.[1]

Another issue raised in the Questionnaire was possible condi-
tioning of grants, the nub of the implied criticism being that
conclusions might be indicated for grantees before grants were
made to them and that acceptance of such conclusions became
a *sine qua non* for a grant. Foundation replies to this question
were a unanimous "no."[2]

In pursuing this tack, Chairman E. E. Cox asked Vannevar
Bush, head of the Carnegie Institution of Washington, if there
was "any disposition on the part of the foundations to so condition their grants as might affect the independence of the
beneficiary." The emphatic reply was, "If there is, Mr. Cox,
I have never seen it. . . ."[3]

Other questions raised in connection with the relative independence of the foundation grantees concerned: (1) withdraw-

---

[1] *Hearings*, Statement of F. Emerson Andrews, p. 40; Frederick Middlebush,
p. 116; Henry M. Wriston, p. 179; Robert M. Hutchins, p. 265; Marshall Field,
p. 450.

[2] *Questionnaire*, sec. E-2a. See p. 133.

[3] *Hearings*, p. 153.

ing support if conclusions at variance with those held by the foundations were reached by the grantees; and (2) the suppression of the findings of the grantees if they differed from the views of the foundation.

Regarding these questions, there was apparent reluctance on the part of some foundations to state their views.[1] Some of them felt that the questions themselves were ambiguous and could not be answered in a clear-cut, concise manner. Others felt that foundation action in these particulars would have to be decided on a case-by-case basis. A majority of the foundations, however, held that in any case where only an honest difference of opinion was involved, aid should not be withdrawn or findings of grantees suppressed. If, on the other hand, the work of the grantee was found to be dishonest, fraudulent, biased, or unscientific, aid could justifiably be withdrawn. Exactly how this judgment as to scientific accuracy and presence or lack of bias was to be made, however, was not clearly indicated. Several of the foundations did mention the use of an impartial panel or board. Suppression, in the sense of destruction of findings, was definitely not favored. It was pointed out, however, that foundations were under no obligation to disseminate or aid in dissemination of findings with which they were in complete disagreement merely because they had made a grant which produced them. It may be noted that the foundations answering these questions with a definite "no" usually followed it with a qualifying "unless there appears misuse of the grant,"[2] or "unless the grant and its purposes are being perverted."[3]

Foundations are understandably reluctant to answer these questions unequivocably. Particular grants and grantees are so variable that it is difficult to state what course of action will be taken in each instance. However, the foundations are probably aware that their own freedom of action, in the last analysis, is dependent upon the independence of their grantees. If too

---

[1] *Questionnaire*, sec. E-2b–c. See p. 133.

[2] M. D. Anderson Foundation, *Answers to Questionnaire*, p. 12.

[3] Twentieth Century Fund, *Answers*, p. 30.

much control, guidance, or call it what you will, is exercised, there would be outcries again, reminiscent of those in the 1920's and 1930's.

Influencing of Public Opinion

In disseminating the information resulting from the aid that they have provided their grantees, the foundations have been placed between Scylla and Charybdis. Operating in diverse ways, with the preventive venture-capital concept that most of them hold, sooner or later some have been accused of using their freedom of action to mold public opinion, and thus indirectly violating the limitations placed on their activities. Of course, it is true that the limitations as set forth in the Internal Revenue Code stipulate that "no substantial part of [their] activities . . . is carrying on propaganda, or otherwise attempting, to influence legislation." Exact definitions of what constitutes a "substantial part," or "propaganda," or "attempting to influence legislation" are hard to come by.

There is a wide difference of opinion on this subject among even the very well informed. The exchange of views between Joseph E. Johnson, head of the Carnegie Endowment for International Peace, and Representative Richard M. Simpson at the 1952 Hearings, for instance, illustrates this divergence. Thus, the activities of the Endowment in sponsoring speakers dealing with the United Nations was defended by the Endowment officer, whereas Representative Simpson, although approving of such activity by the Endowment, felt that it was definitely influencing legislation.[1]

In commenting on this issue of molding opinion, Keppel said that prior to World War I "if any board were unanimous in regarding as socially desirable the spread of a given opinion, there was no hesitation in taking action in supporting this spread." He notes, however, that gradually "it is evident that the realization is coming that while deliberate propagation of opinion is a perfectly legitimate function for the individual, it is

[1] *Hearings*, pp. 591–592.

not the wisest way to use funds that are tax-exempt and therefore 'affected with a public interest.' "[1]

Illustrative of the earlier attitudes, in 1910 Russell Sage Foundation created a Division of Remedial Loans. The director of this Division lobbied in behalf of legislation designed to curb the activity of loan sharks. In some instances, he actually drew up the legislation that put them out of existence.[2]

Even where the motives were undoubtedly blameless, critics felt that the public questioned such action when it was so obviously partisan.[3] Consequently, from World War I on, we find many statements in the annual reports of various foundations that they will not support propaganda or attempt to influence legislation.[4] "Surely," said Keppel, "the discovery and distribution of facts from which men and women may draw their own conclusions offers a field sufficiently wide and sufficiently vital to the welfare of humanity."[5]

Interpretation of what constitutes propaganda or unduly influencing public opinion varies from foundation to foundation. Hollis states that the foundations are confronted with a dilemma. Those "who are afraid of being accused of seeking to influence public opinion run the risk of supporting sterile, academic, fact-finding, 'safe and useless' projects." He concludes that "it is very difficult for trustees to know when they are steering a middle course between these two extremes."[6]

The foundations today are united in opposing direct political activity, propagandizing, or attempts to influence legislation. There is some difference of opinion, however, as to "the influencing of public opinion."[7]

[1] Keppel, Frederick P., The Foundation, p. 46.

[2] Glenn, Brandt, and Andrews, Russell Sage Foundation, 1907–1946, pp. 138–146.

[3] Burns, Allen T., "The Place of Philanthropic Foundations in a Community," Proceedings of the National Conference of Social Work, 1919, pp. 676–678.

[4] Alfred P. Sloan Foundation, Report for 1949–1950, p. 49. Carnegie Corporation of New York, Annual Report, 1924, p. 7; 1939, p. 17; 1944, p. 25; 1945, pp. 15–16. Field Foundation, Annual Report, 1951, p. 39. General Education Board, Annual Report, 1940, p. 159; 1950, p. 55. Rockefeller Foundation, Annual Report, 1917, p. 25; 1941, p. 54; 1943, p. 30.

[5] Carnegie Corporation of New York, Annual Report, 1924, p. 7.

[6] Hollis, Ernest V., Philanthropic Foundations and Higher Education, p. 97.

[7] Questionnaire, sec. E-1, 7. See p. 135.

Twenty-five per cent of the 54 foundations answering the
Select Committee Questionnaire simply declined to answer
this question:

> In your opinion, should educational and philanthropic founda-
> tions and other comparable organizations which are exempt from
> Federal income taxation finance or sponsor projects which may
> have as a direct result the influencing of public opinion in the
> field of politics? Economics? Education? International Relations?
> Religion? Government and Public Administration? Other Fields?
> Explain fully.

They reported that their programs were so limited that they
had not studied the question and, therefore, were not qualified
to render an opinion.

Seven foundations stated flatly that foundations should not
attempt to influence public opinion in any of these fields.
Typical of their replies, although questionable in its interpretation of the limiting wording of the Revenue Code, was the
following:

> No. We believe that the philosophy of the Government which
> directs that charitable foundations, if they are to maintain their
> tax-exempt status, should not seek to influence public opinion, is
> well advised.[1]

The remainder, and a majority, of the foundation answers
to Question E-1 hold that foundations could and should influence public opinion in these fields. Some of their views are
presented verbatim below:

> It is believed that the endowed foundation (of general philan-
> thropic purpose) can render no greater service to its region, its
> nation, or to mankind, than by financing projects designed to
> advance the frontiers of knowledge. Such projects ordinarily call
> for fact-finding by surveys or studies, or for research. These most
> frequently may be found in the social or natural sciences or in
> medicine. Publication of findings is an essential part of such re-
> search. Such publication of new knowledge may, and frequently
> does, influence public opinion, although such influence is likely to
> be indirect rather than direct, long range rather than immediate.

[1] Estate of Harry C. Trexler, *Answers to Questionnaire*, p. 8.

Such seeking out of new knowledge for its own sake and making it available to mankind is conceived to be a high service and an entirely proper use of Foundation funds.

Newly discovered and newly revealed knowledge sometimes leads to the formulation of legislative programs designed to implement this knowledge for the public welfare. This ordinarily calls for an effort to influence public opinion and legislative and administrative opinion *directly*. It is not believed proper to employ Foundation funds in such direct efforts to influence legislation. The Buhl Foundation has made no grants for the purpose of directly influencing public opinion.

It should be pointed out that when a grant is made for a study, survey, or research program it is usually impossible to predict what the findings will be. It is therefore frequently impossible for a Foundation to know when it makes a grant, whether the findings in themselves will have any influence whatever—direct or indirect—on public opinion; nor can it know certainly in advance whether the findings will be of such a nature as to lend themselves to synthesis and the formulation of programs for action.

It is believed that these answers apply, in varying degrees, to all of the classifications listed in this question: politics, economics, education, international relations, religion, and government and public administration.[1]

* * *

Because public opinion on all subjects is formed either by educational or emotional factors, or a combination thereof, it would seem that any support of educational, religious or other charitable organizations would be bound to have either direct or indirect effects in the formation of public opinion. We have made every effort to avoid any activity which might be considered in the "lobbying" category by withholding support from organizations whose sole apparent purpose is to direct public opinion along political lines.[2]

* * *

. . . It is sometimes hard to draw the line between attempts to direct opinion and efforts to make available the facts upon which intelligent public opinion should be based. In general, it is the latter type of activity which the foundation should assist. Thus, it seems unquestionably proper for a foundation to sponsor research which may result in factual findings which will affect

[1] Buhl Foundation, *Answers*, p. 21.
[2] Lilly Endowment, *Answers*, p. 8.

public opinion, or to support an experimental institution, which, if successful, may influence public thinking by its example. Projects of this nature should be independently conducted, with no attempt to impose a predetermined result.[1]

Thus, these foundations feel that any of their activities in these fields mentioned in Question E-1 would, sooner or later, influence public opinion. They hold, however, that such influence is beneficial if exerted in an indirect manner. Moreover, they warned that rigid and fixed interpretation and application of the phrases "propaganda" or "attempting to influence legislation" would probably be disastrous to them.

The findings of the foundations, or their grantees, undoubtedly influence public opinion. Public opinion influences legislation. Therefore, indirectly, the foundations probably do influence legislation. If, on the basis of this reasoning, they were held to be violating the law and forbidden to distribute and disseminate their findings, their effectiveness would be wiped out in one stroke. Thus, restrictions placed upon the foundations at this one point, influencing of opinion, would be turning the clock back two or three centuries. Foundations, as we know them, would drift into sterile adjuncts of the monolithic state.

[1] Old Dominion Foundation, *Answers*, p. 23.

CHAPTER 5

The Public Trust

$\mathbb{F}$OUNDATION donors and officials have consistently recognized the principle of freedom of action as one of their most priceless assets. Yet, in carrying out the preventive venture-capital concept of function they are confronted with a dichotomy that is hard to bridge. As has been noted, the social sciences remain an underdeveloped area where the foundations with their preventive concept of function might be expected to enter. They have entered it. But there has been much questioning of their activities in this area. It is very significant that both congressional investigations of foundations have grown primarily out of their activities, or a misconception of those activities, in the social science field of economics.

The Liberal Criticism

The first congressional investigation of foundations was the United States Senate Industrial Relations Commission of 1915 headed by Senator Frank P. Walsh. This Commission resulted from industrial unrest, culminating in the violent strikes at the Colorado Fuel and Iron Company and the so-called "Ludlow massacre." The Commission's interest in the Rockefeller and other foundations stemmed from the Colorado Fuel and Iron Company's being a Rockefeller corporation and the proposal of the Rockefeller Foundation to investigate industrial relations. The juxtaposition of this proposal to investigate industrial relations and the strife and unrest at Rockefeller plants led many to feel that there was a suspect relationship between the foundations—and the Rockefeller Foundation in particular —and the business interests whose assets they held. Thus, by ostensibly investigating industrial conditions the Rockefeller Foundation might, in reality, be white-washing big business in its controversies with labor. In addition, there was a widespread desire on the part of the Congress and others to ascertain the exact role that philanthropic foundations and trusts were playing in American life.

Many of the witnesses appearing before the Commission were critical of foundations. The dominant theme was that the foundations represented big business and were conservative or even reactionary in their outlook. The entry of foundations into the realm of the social sciences via investigations of industrial relations was deemed ample evidence that they were trying to strengthen the control of big business and the trusts over the American economy by directing or controlling thought. Also, it was feared that this type of activity would lead to foundation control of education. Here again, the fear was expressed that such control would mold education into an ultraconservative pattern.[1] Amos Pinchot described the process:

> Mr. Chairman, I speak advisedly and after some inquiry when I say that the smaller colleges of this country are full of instructors and professors who have not been deliberately driven from larger universities on account of economic opinions unfriendly to benevolent exploiters in industry, but who nevertheless have found their chairs in the large universities untenable, and have left them owing to influences which were irresistible but too subtle to complain about aloud. . . . They [foundations] are providing to the best of their ability, conscientiously if you will but none the

[1] *Industrial Relations:* Final Report and Testimony Submitted to Congress by the Commission on Industrial Relations. U. S. Senate, 64th Congress, 1st Session. Senate Document 415, Government Printing Office, Washington, 1916. Testimony of William H. Allen, vol. 9, pp. 8327–8342; Morris Hillquit, vol. 9, pp. 8262–8286; John Haynes Holmes, vol. 8, pp. 7916–7933; George W. Kirchwey, vol. 9, pp. 8215–8229; John R. Lawson, vol. 8, pp. 8003–8013, vol. 9, pp. 8017–8040; Amos Pinchot, vol. 9, pp. 8041–8052.

less effectively, that our young men in the course of their education shall gain as little understanding as possible of the problems of industrial democracy.[1]

Not sharing these fears, Samuel Untermeyer felt that the foundations were doing "incalculable public good and no harm." His objections were solely organizational. He believed that the foundations should be regulated as to size, income, and type of charter granted them. They should all be chartered by the federal government rather than by the states and there should be government representation on their boards of trustees.[2]

Foundation officials and others connected with them, as might be expected, were of the opinion that there need be no concern about an alleged foundation "menace to American life and education." They felt that adequate reports by the foundations were a sufficient check on their activities. Should the public be dissatisfied with what was being done, remedial action, through their elected representatives, could be effected.[3]

One of these witnesses stated:

> You ask me whether the large resources of endowed foundations constitute a possible menace. In my judgment no concern whatever need be felt on that score, provided the Government will but require that all their transactions, in the minutest detail, be made public once or twice a year. I mean by this a statement showing in detail what their money is invested in, what their income is spent for, and how the fund generally is administered. If in the course of events, under such a system, the money is used for improper purposes, it will not take public opinion long to correct such a condition. I am an absolute believer in the efficiency of public opinion; I believe that nine times out of ten it is not only right but all powerful.[4]

[1] *Ibid.*, Testimony of Amos Pinchot, vol. 9, p. 8048.
[2] *Ibid.*, Testimony of Samuel Untermeyer, vol. 8, pp. 7430–7431.
[3] *Ibid.*, Testimony of Andrew Carnegie, vol. 9, pp. 8286–8297; Charles W. Eliot, vol. 8, pp. 7964–7986; Jerome D. Greene, vol. 9, pp. 8137–8183; George W. Perkins, vol. 8, pp. 7598–7626; John D. Rockefeller, Jr., vol. 8, pp. 7763–7895; John D. Rockefeller, Sr., vol. 9, pp. 8297–8304.
[4] *Ibid.*, Testimony of George W. Perkins, vol. 8, p. 7599.

John D. Rockefeller, Sr., held the same opinion. He regarded

> . . . the right to amend or rescind the respective charters of the several foundations which inhere in the legislative bodies which granted them as an entirely sufficient guarantee against serious abuse of the funds. Furthermore, I have such confidence in democracy that I believe it can better be left to the people and their representatives to remedy the evils when there is some tangible reason for believing they are impending, rather than to restrict the power for service in anticipation of purely hypothetical dangers.[1]

Despite these views, however, the majority report of the Industrial Relations Commission stated that the group controlling industry through the foundations was trying to gain control of the universities and thereby the social and educational side of American life. It was pointed out that the Rockefeller and Carnegie foundations alone wielded an income twice as great as federal expenditures for education and social services. This wealth was the result of overpricing products to the consumer and the exploitation of the American worker; it was exempt from taxation, subject to the dictates of the donors during their lives, and completely free of public control. Since this wealth represented holdings in American business corporations, inevitably foundations would reflect the corporate or big business outlook. Therefore, the entrance of foundations into the field of industrial relations constituted a definite menace to the welfare of the country. The report recommended that: (a) limitations be placed on the size, income, and life of those foundations with over one million dollars in assets; (b) the federal government should step up its appropriations for education and social welfare.[2]

The interpretation of the liberals that foundations were a force for reaction and conservatism appears to have been accepted well into the 1930's. For instance, one observer, commenting on philanthropy and philanthropists in particular, stated:

[1] *Ibid.*, Testimony of John D. Rockefeller, Sr., vol. 9, p. 8298.
[2] *Ibid.*, vol. 1, pp. 5–269.

The philanthropists belong to a class on which the injustices of our present basis of society have not borne heavily. They serve unconsciously as a bulwark of the *status quo*, for whose defects they are ready and eager to apply palliatives. They are the great menders and patchers-up of society, not the surgeons who cut deep into the festering sore and scrape the bone.[1]

Lindeman, in 1936, explained that, while foundations were not an actual conspiracy on the part of the guardians of vested wealth:

> More accurate would be the statement that these vested funds represent a consistently conservative element in our civilization, and that wherever their appropriations are accepted there enters at the same time this subtle influence in the direction of protecting the value system in existence, that is, of conserving the *status quo*.

He concluded that so long as the philanthropic foundations and trusts were privately managed and controlled little else could be expected.[2]

Coffman's study drew much the same conclusions.[3] Though admitting prevalence of the belief in the conservative bent of the foundations, Hollis felt that many were progressive or liberal. He cited the influence of the foundations in the support of progressive education and experimental college programs as proof of his argument.[4]

What was the foundation attitude during the decades following the Walsh Commission investigation?

Possibly because of the stir the investigation produced but also because of the changed economic conditions following World War I, the Rockefeller Foundation, in 1918, dropped the projected study of industrial relations.[5] Annual reports of several of the largest foundations, however, show that there

---

[1] Cannon, Cornelia J., "Philanthropic Doubts," *Atlantic Monthly*, vol. 128, September, 1921, p. 294.

[2] Lindeman, Eduard C., *Wealth and Culture*, pp. 12, 58.

[3] Coffman, Harold C., *American Foundations*, p. 30.

[4] Hollis, Ernest V., *Philanthropic Foundations and Higher Education*, pp. 58–64.

[5] Rockefeller Foundation, *Annual Report*, 1918, pp. 50–52.

was still a conviction of the great need for research and study in the social science field.[1]

As early as 1936, Keppel posed the question as to whether or not man had reached the point where he had more control over nature than himself. He wondered if "science and industry can hardly dare to go very much farther in wresting secrets from nature before we are confident that mankind as a whole can be trusted with them." To him, this problem was the great challenge of the future. He warned that successful solutions would depend, not on the number of people working in the field, but on their quality.[2]

In a chapter prophetically titled "Frankenstein," Fosdick questioned whether our technology could be brought under control before we blotted out civilization. He warned of the urgency of the situation:

> This, then, is the problem—far more immediate and acute today than it was twenty years ago. It cannot complacently be left to time to solve. We cannot count on geologic ages for the development of methods of social control. What we do in this generation and the next may well decide the kind of civilization, if any, which is to dominate the globe for centuries to come.[3]

The various social science projects and programs inaugurated by the foundations in the period from World War I to World War II still met with opposition, however. It was distinguished from that which had precipitated the Walsh Commission in that it came from both liberal and conservative elements. Keppel urged the foundations to stay in the field despite these criticisms, counseling that they should "take comfort in the fact that studies in controversial fields which they support are usually attacked with equal ardor from the left and from the right."[4] Embree feared that, rather than causing subversion to the right or left, the foundations would have no

[1] Carnegie Corporation of New York, *Annual Report*, 1923, pp. 32–34. Laura Spelman Rockefeller Memorial, *Final Report*, 1933, pp. 8–9. Rockefeller Foundation, *Annual Report*, 1936, pp. 7–8; 1939, pp. 44–57; 1940, pp. 249–278.
[2] Keppel, Frederick P., *Philanthropy and Learning*, p. 36.
[3] Rockefeller Foundation, *Annual Report*, 1943, pp. 26–28.
[4] Keppel, Frederick P., *Philanthropy and Learning*, p. 29.

influence whatever and would fritter away their resources in ineffectual projects. His real concern was the growth of foundation bureaucrats "fat in posts."[1]

The great depression of the 1930's, of course, accented this difference between the "right" and the "left." Foundation officials recommended that the foundations should not take "sides." It was felt that this controversy was temporary and sooner or later a middle way would evolve. As a result of the depression and other world events, the government would play a larger role in all aspects of American life. It would be a mistake, however, to bring everything under state control. Quite fittingly, private philanthropy was cited as an example of something that must be exempted.[2]

The Conservative Reaction

The second investigation of foundations grew partially out of the differences between "right" and "left," mentioned above, and partially out of various problems which were an aftermath of World War II.

In particular, the United States, confronted with the problem of traitors and subversives within its own borders to an extent never existing before, sought the reasons. What would cause the well-bred and educated, those who stood to benefit most from our way of life, to embrace communism? Was our educational system at fault? Was it at fault in its interpretation or conduct of the social sciences, and of economics and economic history particularly?

In a search for the answers to these and related questions, inevitably interested persons would attempt to assay the role played by the foundations. In view of their importance in the educational world, the diversity and range of their operations, their freedom of action, their venture-capital concept, it is understandable that a spotlight would be turned on them.

[1] Embree, Edwin R., "The Business of Giving Away Money," *Harper's Magazine*, vol. 161, August, 1930, p. 329.

[2] Flexner, Abraham, "Private Fortunes and the Public Future," *Atlantic Monthly*, vol. 156, August, 1935, pp. 215–224. See also Carnegie Corporation of New York, *Annual Report*, 1935, pp. 38–40.

A Select Committee was created on April 4, 1952, by House Resolution 561, Eighty-second Congress, Second Session. In the words of its architect, Representative E. E. Cox of Georgia, this Committee was

> . . . authorized and directed to conduct a full and complete investigation and study of educational and philanthropic foundations and other comparable organizations which are exempt from Federal income taxation to determine which such foundations and organizations are using their resources for purposes other than the purposes for which they were established and especially to determine which such foundations and organizations are using their resources for un-American and subversive activities or for purposes not in the interest or tradition of the United States.[1]

From the wording of this resolution, it can be seen that the Select Committee was given a broad range in its investigative activities. Consequently, it approached the investigation on the same basis. While cognizant that it was specifically charged with the duty of investigating the foundations for "un-American or subversive activities," it also realized that it was expected to conduct "a full and complete investigation and study." The merit of its attempt is attested by the published *Hearings* and the *Final Report* of this Committee and the extensive research which was a partial basis for those documents.

While attention was given to the number and size of foundations, their rate of growth, their relative role in modern society, and their present and future need, particular attention was given to the criticisms leveled at foundations, which, in large measure, had spurred the investigation. Although there were others, "the criticism most frequently made against foundations and . . . the one urged with the greatest vehemence" was:

> Have foundations supported or assisted persons, organizations, and projects which, if not subversive in the extreme sense of the word, tend to weaken or discredit the capitalistic system as it exists in the United States and to favor Marxist socialism?[2]

[1] *Final Report of the Select Committee to Investigate Foundations and Other Organizations.* U. S. House, 82d Congress, 2d Session. House Report 2514, Government Printing Office, Washington, 1953, p. 2.

[2] *Ibid.*, p. 9.

Before attempting to analyze the answers to this question, which was put to a score of witnesses at the Select Committee Hearings, it may be well to throw some perspective on the relative amount, kind, and manner of activity of foundations in the fields of economics, and government and public administration. Since these facets of the social sciences seem to bear directly on the question of subversion, that portion of the Questionnaire which deals with them should prove enlightening.[1]

The first thing that strikes one is the relative scarcity of foundations operating directly in these fields. Of course, many of the foundations indirectly sponsor research and studies in economics, and government and public administration by supporting educational and other institutions which do engage in such work. But the fact remains that only seven foundations operated or made grants directly in the field of economics and only seven in the government and public administration field. The foundations so engaged made extensive use of consultants in an attempt to gain as broad a base as possible for the making of grants.

As in other programs, no attempts were made to present divergent views, as such, in these fields. The General Education Board, for instance, explained that it would be difficult to disentangle the purely economic from its educational program, but it felt that the colleges and universities which it supported would "provide opportunities for discussion of all valid points relating to controversial issues."[2]

The Twentieth Century Fund, which is one of the very few foundations operating solely in the social science field, stated:

No effort is made to assist or support individuals, groups or projects representing divergent views as such. In organizing the special committees which review the research done in each project, and formulate conclusions and recommendations, attempt is made to secure representation of divergent points of view where there is recognized divergence of opinion. Where, as a

[1] *Questionnaire*, sec. E-5, 6. See pp. 134–135.
[2] General Education Board, *Answers to Questionnaire*, p. 97.

result, agreement is reached, this is published; where the parties disagree, note of disagreement commonly appears in the published study.[1]

The foundations felt that it was difficult to answer questions about the effect of their activities in these fields. Their total work was so wide and the indirect effects so manifold that, on the whole, only two could possibly be pointed to as direct effects: (1) the growth of a body of factual knowledge, such as the size and distribution of the national income, which has been widely used by government and industry; and (2) the development of skilled personnel in these fields who are likely to be precise and scientific rather than dogmatic in their work. Basis for this belief appears to be summarized in the Rockefeller Foundation policy statement on economics, which follows:

> In supporting work in economics, The Rockefeller Foundation has been influenced, first of all, by the desire to strengthen efforts to make the study of economics a genuinely scientific one and not one based merely on theoretical deduction or personal preferences. In doing this, the Foundation has sought to have its funds go to those who work with scientific care, competence, and responsibility, wherever they may be. The Foundation has sought to strengthen the efforts of those who are building a body of definitely ascertained fact on the basis of which useful scholarship and expert teaching may rest with greater confidence.[2]

Approximately a score of foundation witnesses at the Hearings before the Select Committee were asked whether or not the foundations were sponsoring or supporting projects or studies that tended to undermine or weaken the capitalistic or free enterprise system. Unanimously, they were of the opinion that, rather than undermining the system, foundation activities in economics and other areas tended to strengthen and help it.[3]

[1] Twentieth Century Fund, *Answers*, p. 39.

[2] Rockefeller Foundation, *Answers*, p. 116.

[3] *Hearings*, Statement of William I. Myers, pp. 129, 137, 139–140; Vannevar Bush, p. 151; Henry M. Wriston, p. 183; Paul G. Hoffman, pp. 256–257; Robert M. Hutchins, pp. 286–287; Charles Dollard, p. 354; Russell C. Leffingwell, p. 378; Donald Young, p. 400; Alfred P. Sloan, Jr., p. 462; John D. Rockefeller III, p. 568; Joseph E. Johnson, p. 595.

The president of Brown University, Henry M. Wriston, explained that, while many of the economic studies and projects were critical of the capitalistic system, he felt capitalism thrived on a "drumfire of criticism." Such criticism, if justified, could be utilized to correct any excesses or abuses in the system and thereby keep it strong and vigorous.[1]

An apt illustration of Wriston's statement was offered by Vannevar Bush, president of the Carnegie Institution of Washington. He pointed out that our country has a very good, private medical system. England, on the other hand, has a socialized system. Bush felt that one of the reasons we avoided this expedient was early foundation activity in, and ofttimes criticism of, the field of medicine.[2]

Alfred P. Sloan, Jr., one of America's foremost living industrialists and creator of a large foundation, in replying to the question of possible subversion, introduced a personal note into the Hearings:

> I have taken out of this system certain property because I have been fortunate, Mr. Keele, in being connected with successful enterprises. I put back into the foundation what I have taken out, to strengthen and develop the system. That point of view must prevail in the minds of all individuals who have accumulated property and who create these foundations.
>
> They have enjoyed a great benefit in this system. What they have in the world has come out of the system. It is impossible to assume that knowingly they would do anything to destroy the very system by which they have profited.[3]

As a result of this and other testimony, plus extensive research, the Select Committee concluded that the foundations had not used their resources to discredit or undermine the capitalistic system, nor had they used them to advance Marxist socialism. In its *Final Report* the Committee stated:

> It seems paradoxical that in a previous congressional investigation in 1915 the fear most frequently expressed was that the foun-

[1] *Ibid.*, Statement of Henry M. Wriston, p. 183.
[2] Statement of Vannevar Bush, p. 151.
[3] *Ibid.*, Statement of Alfred P. Sloan, Jr., p. 462.

dations would prove the instruments of vested wealth, privilege, and reaction, while today the fear most frequently expressed is that they have become the enemy of the capitalistic system. In our opinion neither of these fears is justified.[1]

The Committee also devoted considerable attention to the other major subversive questions: infiltration of the foundations and obtaining of grants from the foundations by communists. One complete section of the Questionnaire, Section D, was devoted to such questions. Several other sections bore on these in varying degrees. Virtually all the witnesses appearing before the Select Committee were queried regarding subversive activities.

From a consideration of the evidence submitted, the Committee concluded that, with a few notable exceptions such as Alger Hiss, communists or communist sympathizers had not attained influential positions in any of the foundations, large or small. Although agreeing that the communists had obtained some grants from the large foundations, the Committee stated:

> In the aggregate, the number of such grants and the amounts involved are alarming. Proportionately, when viewed in the light of the total grants made, they are surprisingly small.[2]

In support of this conclusion the Rockefeller Foundation may be cited as an example. While it made over 6,000 grants to individuals for fellowships since it began operations, only two had been cited by the House Un-American Activities Committee. Eleven other persons who benefited in some way from Foundation grants were also cited by the Committee, but these grants with one exception were all made to institutions rather than directly to the individuals concerned.[3] Looking at the question from another angle, it can be noted that, of the 54 larger foundations, only nine had made grants to individuals or organizations cited by the House Un-American Activities Committee or by the Subcommittee on Internal Security of the

[1] *Final Report of the Select Committee to Investigate Foundations and Other Organizations,* p. 10.

[2] *Ibid.,* p. 7.

[3] Rockefeller Foundation, *Answers to Questionnaire,* pp. 64–67.

Judiciary Committee of the United States Senate. And, in each instance, those cited comprised a relative handful out of the thousands of grantees.[1]

Therefore, the final conclusion was this:

> The committee believes that on balance the record of the foundations is good. It believes that there was infiltration and that judgments were made which, in the light of hindsight, were mistakes, but it also believes that many of these mistakes were made without the knowledge of facts which, while later obtainable, could not have been readily ascertained at the time decisions were taken.[2]

The Public Trust

Many of the foundations have embraced the principle of the public trust, perhaps partially as a result of these investigations. The basic premise is that since foundation endowments are tax exempt on the basis of devotion to the public welfare, foundations have a responsibility to the public to operate as wisely and efficiently as possible. A feasible method of assuring the public of this is publication of periodic reports.

The annual reports of the Carnegie and Rockefeller groups, published since their inception, are voluminous evidence of their belief in the principle of reporting activities. Frequently, especially in recent reports, there are references to a belief that foundations are affected with a public interest. Public confidence in the foundations, it is stated, rests on knowledge of their activities. It is repeatedly urged, therefore, that more foundations publish periodic reports.[3]

Keppel, in 1930 and in 1936, warned the foundations that they

> . . . should certainly have learned by this time, but some of us act as if we hadn't, that our present exemption from taxation rests wholly upon public confidence, upon the confidence that

---

[1] *Questionnaire*, sec. D-14, 15. See p. 132.

[2] *Final Report of the Select Committee to Investigate Foundations and Other Organizations*, p. 8.

[3] For example, see Carnegie Corporation of New York, *Annual Report*, 1929, pp. 23–24; 1931, p. 28; 1934, pp. 39–40.

what we are doing is worth while, and upon evidence that it is done openly and in the sight of all men.[1]

Scholars working in the foundation field, however, have stated that many foundations feel that their activities are solely a private concern and that they have no inherent responsibility to inform the public of their actions.[2]

Lindeman, consistent with his interpretation of foundations as a bulwark of the reactionaries, held that a sense of social responsibility was not a normal thought-pattern of the possessors of great wealth. He asserted:

> On the whole they and their administrators continue to insist that wealth is a private possession and that the possessor may dispose of it as he pleases. This attitude characterizes the administration of most of our American foundations. In spite of the fact that these are semi-public institutions, and that their influence upon American civilization is one of profound proportions, officials of foundations are distinctly unwilling to furnish facts to investigators and thus to the public.

He admitted, however, that a small minority showed the opposite attitude, readily responding to requests for information on their activities.[3]

Hollis agrees that many foundations were unwilling to divulge information. He believes, however, that it may be due to reasons other than a desire to be secretive. He points out that some foundations are incorporations of private charity, which are understandably reticent about their work lest they be accused of bragging; a certain amount of jealousy exists; foundations object to being practiced on by neophyte graduate students; and, finally, any publicity, in a day of mass journalism, brings a flood of appeals for aid.[4]

[1] Keppel, Frederick P., *Philanthropy and Learning*, pp. 170–171. See also Keppel, *The Foundation*, pp. 56–57; and Lester, Robert E., "The Philanthropic Endowment in Modern Life," *South Atlantic Quarterly*, vol. 34, January, 1935, p. 12.

[2] Coffman, Harold C., *American Foundations*, p. 7; Hollis, Ernest V., *Philanthropic Foundations and Higher Education*, pp. 68–75; Lindeman, Eduard C., *Wealth and Culture*, p. vii.

[3] Lindeman, Eduard C., *Wealth and Culture*, pp. 5–6.

[4] Hollis, Ernest V., *Philanthropic Foundations and Higher Education*, pp. 8–9.

As has been mentioned in a previous section, several witnesses testifying in the first congressional investigation urged full public disclosure by the foundations of their activities. They reasoned that this was the best possible answer to critics.[1]

Despite such urging and the criticisms leveled at foundations, it is only recently that many foundations have published reports of their activities.

Information furnished the public in state and federal reports has also been meagre and hard to get. It is, of course, true that foundations and philanthropic trusts tax exempt under Section 162(a) of the Internal Revenue Code have always been required to make an annual income-tax return, but the government has not segregated these from the returns of other trusts.

Furthermore, not until 1943 do we find a law that specifies that organizations exempt under Section 101 must file a more comprehensive report. The relative efficacy of this reporting, however, is doubtful. Since the follow-up procedure is inadequate, it is most improbable that all tax-exempt foundations file reports. Also, only a sampling technique is used in ascertaining their accuracy and veracity.[2]

Foundation witnesses before the 1952 Investigating Committee not only urged a better system of official reporting; they repeatedly expressed the belief that foundations were public trusts and therefore had a moral, if not legal, obligation to make the fullest possible disclosure of their activities to the public. Repeated references were made to the fact that they should operate in a "goldfish bowl."

Views were also expressed that foundation reports should not be merely a mass of statistics. They should be readable and go into the theories or principles on which the particular foundation operated. Too, many thought foundations should explain, at least in a limited way, why they made particular grants. While admitting that present law did require some reporting, several witnesses testified that reports furnished pur-

[1] See p. 87.
[2] *Hearings*, Statement of Norman A. Sugarman, pp. 55–82.

suant to it were inadequate in scope and content.[1] Thus,
Donald Young, general director of Russell Sage Foundation,
maintained:

> You ought to give not only the bare facts but you ought to give
> your reasons, your philosophy, for working into the kind of pro-
> gram that you have in operation.
>
> In addition, there should be a record of who are the trustees,
> who are the staff, what is the field of operation; in other words,
> what are you trying to do; what means are you taking to accom-
> plish the objectives, what kind of projects are you engaged in, and
> even why do you try these projects.[2]

Such reporting, it was argued, would not place an undue
burden on the foundations. For, presumably, the smaller foundations would have less to report while the larger ones would
have larger staffs to handle the job.[3]

Another witness pointed out the difficulty of present access
to foundation reports. An Executive Order would be required
to see all the reports filed in Washington. Under certain restrictions, duplicates are available to the public, but they are
scattered in 60 or 70 district Internal Revenue offices.

The assembling of these reports in a central place where
they would be easily accessible to the public, therefore, was
felt to be a necessity.[4]

In arguing the validity of official reporting, Chester I.
Barnard, a former president of the Rockefeller Foundation,
stated that trusts which were not tax exempt were required, in
the public interest, to file reports. He saw no reason for not
making the same requirement of those which were tax exempt.[5]

The principle of the public trust was probably uppermost in
the minds of those foundation officials urging the necessity of
public reporting. They also felt that if enough people could be

---

[1] *Hearings*, Statement of Vannevar Bush, pp. 155–156; Paul G. Hoffman,
p. 252; Donald Young, pp. 389–390; Malcolm Pratt Aldrich, p. 405; Michael
Whitney Straight, p. 412; Milton C. Rose, p. 419; Marshall Field, p. 440; Alfred
P. Sloan, Jr., p. 454; Dean Rusk, pp. 501–504; Joseph E. Johnson, pp. 574–575.

[2] *Ibid.*, Statement of Donald Young, p. 390.

[3] *Ibid.*, Statement of Marshall Field, p. 440.

[4] *Ibid.*, Statement of F. Emerson Andrews, pp. 22, 49.

[5] *Ibid.*, Statement of Chester I. Barnard, pp. 557–558.

made aware of what the larger foundations were doing it would halt the criticism based on the belief that foundations are great, amorphous organizations conducting their operations in a veiled, mysterious manner.

The heads of two of the largest foundations stated that they made strenuous efforts to keep the public informed of their activities. Thus, in addition to the required official reports, they prepared and distributed elaborate brochures detailing their doings.[1] One of these officials felt, moreover, that what had been done in the past was not enough and that his foundation was stepping up its efforts to inform the public.[2]

Concerning the attitude of the larger foundations on these principles of the public trust and public reporting the 1952 House Select Committee reported:

> The larger foundations take the position that as public trusts they are accountable to the public and that the public is entitled to know in detail about their resources, income, expenditures, personnel, and programs. Stated in the words of one of their trustees "foundations should not only operate in a goldfish bowl— they should operate with glass pockets." In short the larger foundations favor public accountability and public accounting.[3]

Foundation opinion was divided on the rationale for public accountability. One group emphasized that foundation funds were used for the public welfare; therefore, the public had an interest in the manner of their disposal. In this connection, comparisons to colleges and universities were drawn. Such reasoning is voiced by the Commonwealth Fund. It stated:

> Foundations are instruments of society for advancing social progress and are responsible, broadly speaking, to society for their performance. The public must know what foundations are doing in order to judge them intelligently.[4]

[1] *Ibid.*, Statement of H. Rowan Gaither, Jr., p. 205; Charles Dollard, p. 346.
[2] *Ibid.*, Statement of Charles Dollard, p. 346.
[3] *Final Report of the Select Committee to Investigate Foundations and Other Organizations*, pp. 12–13.
[4] Commonwealth Fund, *Answers to Questionnaire*, p. 33.

Another group pointed to the tax-exemption privilege as the rationale for their belief in public accounting. Since the foundations enjoyed special government consideration in the matter of taxation, they were affected with a public interest. As stated by the Houston Endowment,

> . . . the public has a direct interest in tax-exempt foundations and comparable organizations for the basic and fundamental reason that when it votes these tax-exempt foundations into this favored status, thereby assuming the additional tax burden from which they are relieved, then it has an uncontrovertible right to determination that the favored entity honestly pursues its declared intention.[1]

Several of the foundations combined these reasons. The Old Dominion Foundation observed:

> . . . the public has a direct interest in tax-exempt foundations and comparable organizations for two principal reasons. The fields which foundations support, such as education, religion, and health, are themselves of direct interest to the public; and the public has an interest to see that the tax exemption granted by it through government is not abused.[2]

In specifying the degree of government regulation necessary to implement this principle of the public trust, the foundations were unanimously of the opinion that the least possible degree of government supervision was best. Thus, a purely passive form of government regulation was deemed the most desirable method, and government supervision of public reporting by the foundation the best means to achieve this goal.

Approximately 50 per cent of the foundations felt that existing regulations were adequate. They favored stricter applications of the regulations and urged greater effort by the foundations themselves to implement the concept of the public trust. The Carnegie Corporation of New York, for example, stated that the existing Internal Revenue Code already provided for the filing of information. This foundation felt that it was still

[1] Houston Endowment, *Answers*, p. 46.
[2] Old Dominion Foundation, *Answers*, p. 38.

too early to tell whether this recently enacted law was adequate or not. It pointed out that at least 12 foundations have voluntarily begun to issue comprehensive annual reports since 1950. Thus, it would be unwise to pass new legislation until that already in existence had been given a fair trial. In the meantime, the foundations themselves could make increased efforts toward self-publicizing.[1]

The John and Mary R. Markle Foundation said:

> Free foundations to be worth while must remain as free as possible of government regulation so they may change programs as the public needs change and be in a position to pioneer. Any government regulations should be held to an absolute minimum, should be confined to control of abuses of these privileges, should encourage the publication of public reports of their activities and should prevent the funds from being used for other than charitable, educational and scientific purposes.[2]

On the other hand, another large group of the foundations felt that existing regulations were inadequate as regards the provisions for public reporting. Although cognizant that many of the larger foundations were already making their activities a matter of public record, they felt that, in order to gain complete and continuing public confidence for foundations as a whole, it should be mandatory for all foundations to make comprehensive official reports. Furthermore, there should be more active inspection of these reports to determine that all was well in the operation of the foundations. The views of Russell Sage Foundation typify the feelings of this group. It stated:

> A program to ensure accountability for all foundations might include:
> 1. A registry of all foundations and charitable trusts. (Presumably through uniform legislation in all the states, under the laws of which such organizations are usually originated. The registry should be public, segregated, and kept current.)

[1] Carnegie Corporation of New York, *Answers*, pp. 62–63.
[2] John and Mary R. Markle Foundation, *Answers*, p. 25.

2. Compulsory annual reporting, including a full financial statement and a description of activities. (These reports should be open to the public. To some extent this purpose is already accomplished on the federal level through compulsory filing of Form 990A.)

3. Provision for regular review of such reports by a public authority possessing power to correct abuses. (Presumably such power resides in the states which were the constituting authorities, and would be exercised through the office of the respective attorneys general.)

The Foundation immediately followed this proposal, however, with a warning paragraph.

These measures do not envisage control of program, which is regarded as unwarranted and dangerous. The mere existence of power to divert such funds into only such channels as might receive wide public support at a given moment would both discourage new gifts of thoughtful donors and threaten the essential ingredient in the success of the foundation movement—freedom to experiment.[1]

This note of warning was echoed in a greater or lesser degree by all of the foundations. Thus, the El Pomar Foundation warned against any excessive regulatory measures.

While some reasonable governmental regulation might have a possible value, nevertheless if such regulation was attempted it would sooner or later result in a complete control and occupation of the field, which would be disastrous. . . . Experience in other branches of government activities fully justified that statement.[2]

When questioned as to whether or not they felt that "any limits should be placed on educational and philanthropic foundations and comparable organizations as to the size of endowment, legal life, right of trustees to spend its capital funds, etc.," the answer was an emphatic "no."[3]

Some warned that imposition of such restrictions would curtail or possibly stop the creation of new foundations. Others

[1] Russell Sage Foundation, *Answers*, pp. 23–24.
[2] El Pomar Foundation, *Answers*, pp. 26–27.
[3] *Questionnaire*, sec. G-9. See p. 137.

stated that in a country as large as the United States, with its great diversity in both the physical and intellectual sense, there was plenty of room for a diversity of foundations. Thus, the variety of foundations resulting from the varying views of many creators was felt to be beneficial. Although admitting that the operations of some foundations might be improved by the imposition of various restrictions, the net result, it was feared, would be a loss. Finally, it was noted, no one had proved that the lack of such restrictions had worked evil. In the words of the Ford Foundation:

> While opinions differ whether the most effective contribution comes from a foundation with a limited or unlimited life, or with the right to invade capital funds, there has not, in our opinion, been any showing of inherent evil in unlimited size of endowment, unlimited legal life, or unlimited right of trustees to spend capital funds. We believe, therefore, that these are freedoms which may properly be left to the foundations.[1]

Although there are some notable exceptions, it appears, therefore, that the belief of foundations that they are a public trust and should report their activities to the public, is a relatively late development. It seems to have emerged as the answer to those who are critical of foundations, also because of a growing recognition by the foundations themselves that their tax-exemption privilege implies a responsibility to the public.

This public trust characteristic emphasizes the desirability of the three previously discussed principles: diversity of operation; preventive venture-capital function; and freedom of action. Yet, by espousing the public trust aspect with its corollary of public accountability or reporting, the foundations are confronted with the danger of all-out public, that is, governmental regulation and control in the areas delineated by the three basic principles. Apparently a majority of foundations are ready to brave the dangers inherent in this course, relying on publicity and the good sense of the American people. For the foundations realize that unless the public recognizes and helps to maintain their basic freedom, foundations will perish.

[1] Ford Foundation, *Answers*, p. 69.

CHAPTER 6

Evaluation and Conclusion

P AST AND PRESENT foundation heads have stated that a main difficulty facing any foundation is not adverse criticism but a lack of it.[1] Lack of knowledge and interest on the part of the public in foundation affairs is partly responsible. Too, those who live in lively anticipation of foundation favors are understandably loath to give forthright, unbiased, constructive criticism. This relative scarcity of criticism, however, serves to highlight whatever does emerge.

Mistakes and Difficulties

Criticism of foundations, probably more than other American cultural and philanthropic institutions, is based on relative judgments. Even foundation heads, in attempting to explain the application or misapplication of foundation principles, are forced to rely on what they call "feel" or "touch."[2] For example, the most frequently alleged mistake and, consequently, one of the most difficult problems for the foundations, has been the tendency of their system of operation to place

[1] For example, see Keppel, Frederick P., *The Foundation*, p. 30; and *Hearings*, Statement of Charles Dollard, pp. 346–347.

[2] *Hearings*, Statement of Henry Allen Moe, p. 618; *Appreciations of Frederick Paul Keppel* by Some of His Friends, Columbia University Press, New York, 1951, pp. 58–59.

"restriction on the spontaneity, independence, and variety of productive scholarship."[1] However, if the foundations exercise no degree of control there is ample evidence that their grants would soon degenerate into mere handouts. Conversely, if too much control is exercised, grantees or prospective grantees might become fawning sycophants. Consequently, while admittedly this question of control is a major difficulty in foundation operation, it largely resolves itself into a problem that can be solved only by the operating skill and finesse of foundation officials. Procedures and rules will not provide the solution. Too, the kind and degree of control would vary greatly owing to the variety of purposes for which foundations operate. Thus, the differences in control exercised by the institutional and operating types are obvious. The fellowship type would call for still another method.

Viewed in a relative way, criticisms and alleged mistakes arise from the difficulties that face most foundations, and can only be solved by wise administration. A cataloguing of some of these criticisms, however, may bring these difficulties into clearer focus.

One of the most trenchant, biting criticisms of foundations, and incidentally of our universities and political system, was voiced by Harold Laski.[2] Boiled down to a few words, Laski seemed to say to foundations: look for the talented individual; reduce the amount of red tape; eliminate research for research's sake. Essentially, he said, the foundation job is to spot, as early as possible, the relatively few really able men. The problem is how to dig them out from under the bureaucratic and administrative rocks that clutter the intellectual landscape. At a time when foundations are placing increasing emphasis on social and humanistic programs, it would be well for foundation executives to consider this criticism.

In his 1936 study, Lindeman summarized the criticisms appearing in a selected group of weekly and monthly periodicals.

[1] Ogg, Frederick A., *Research in the Humanistic and Social Sciences*. Century Co., New York, 1928, p. 330.
[2] Laski, Harold, *The Dangers of Obedience and Other Essays*. Harper and Bros., New York, 1930, pp. 150–177.

It is necessary to bear in mind that this study was based on small as well as large foundations and included community trusts. The extent to which it applies to the larger foundations, therefore, is conjectural. Lindeman's conclusions indicate that the bulk of criticism was directed against the foundation donor or official for being short-sighted or emotional and impulsive in his giving. Other criticisms were occasional jealousies between foundations and an emphasis on palliative rather than preventive giving.[1]

As the result of various confidential foundation reports, Coffman listed 14 mistakes to which foundation officials themselves stated they were prone. These rather vague and overlapping points can be reduced to the following:

1. Programs—not well-defined, static, impulsive, perfunctory, palliative, neglectful of certain needed programs.

2. Officers and trustees—drawn from too narrow a group; dangers of self-perpetuation.

3. Control—stifling of change in dependent organizations; influencing public opinion; too much exercised in directing research.

4. Public trust—responsibility to public not recognized, as indicated by failure to issue reports.[2]

A criticism made by Edwin F. Embree was that foundations suffer from timidity. As a contrast to present-day mediocrity, he pointed to the bold programs of fifty years ago in such fields as medicine and education. In elaborating on this theme, Embree spoke of:

1. Scatteration giving, that is, "the sprinkling of little grants over a multiplicity of causes and institutions."

2. Bureaucracy and traditionalism which result in many safe programs and few new ventures.

3. Too great a concern with conservation of resources; this criticism was closely tied in with the preceding.

[1] Lindeman, Eduard C., *Wealth and Culture*, p. 53.
[2] Coffman, Harold C., *American Foundations*, pp. 65–66.

4. Abuses of the tax-exemption privilege by some organizations, coupled with a failure or refusal to divulge information.[1]

Here, as in the Lindeman and Coffman studies, we find that many of these criticisms or alleged mistakes are relative and arguable points. For instance, in the case of scatteration giving, although admitting there was a degree of validity in the criticism, a foundation witness appearing before the 1952 Select Committee pointed out that the discovery of insulin came about largely as the result of a $9,000 foundation grant to Dr. Banting. Also, the revolution in American medicine effected by the Flexner Report was mentioned. This Report cost a little less than $10,000. Thus, other factors, such as timing, were held to be as important as, if not more important than, the size of grants.[2]

When questioned as to their views on the mistakes foundations had made, foundation heads offered a varied set of answers.[3] Several mentioned such nontheoretical items as undue accumulation of funds and clumsy or restrictive construction of the charters or legal instruments creating some foundations as chief mistakes. Others designated such relative or arguable items as: scatteration giving, slowness in action, not recognizing the public interest in foundation activities. The period of support was seen as a problem. The Milbank Memorial Fund felt that foundations often made the mistake of not supporting "research projects for sufficiently long periods . . . too many foundations support such projects on a year to year basis, whereas many projects need the assurance of support for a period of years."[4] The Commonwealth Fund maintained that one of the chief foundation mistakes was "clinging too long to a program whose essential educational effect has been

---

[1] Embree, Edwin C., "Are the Foundations Doing Their Job?" *Harper's Magazine*, vol. 198, March, 1949, pp. 28–37. See also Flexner, Abraham, *Funds and Foundations*, pp. 77–88.

[2] *Hearings*, Statement of Charles Dollard, p. 349.

[3] *Questionnaire*, sec. G-3c. See p. 136.

[4] Milbank Memorial Fund, *Answers to Questionnaire*, p. 36.

achieved,"[1] but recognized that long-range support was often justified.

Two nonrelated mistakes were most often emphasized. The first deals with a human problem and penetrates to the heart of foundation giving. Perhaps, as a mistake, it can be corrected only by the development of that "feel" or "touch" mentioned by Keppel and Moe. In any event, the kernel of this belief is that most foundation mistakes are due to errors in judgment concerning the significance and promise of men, projects, and institutions receiving grants, plus the timing and manner in which grants are made. The Carnegie Corporation of New York stated it in these words:

> The mistakes that foundations make derive from the same limitations of human nature that are responsible for the mistakes of other organizations, both private and public. These limitations are fallible judgment about the capacities of people and institutions and less-than-perfect foresight as to future developments. Other mistakes arise from bad timing and bad planning. A grant can come too soon or too late to have maximum effect. Looking only at the Corporation's record, sometimes it would have been better if we had put our money on one man instead of distributing it among five. Sometimes hindsight indicates that we were overcautious; occasionally we have acted too quickly. We are continually reviewing past programs so as to improve future decisions.[2]

The other mistake that was believed to be most prevalent was a disinclination or reluctance to enter experimental or controversial fields. It was asserted that foundations had, particularly in the past but still much too much in the present, placed too great emphasis on "brick and mortar" programs and "made too few bold marches in new fields of progress, not available to individual finance."[3] Thus, many were still supporting programs which already had or should have ample public support via taxation. Institutions such as orphanages and old-age homes quickly leap to mind as illustrations.

[1] Commonwealth Fund, *Answers*, p. 32.
[2] Carnegie Corporation of New York, *Answers*, p. 60.
[3] Kresge Foundation, *Answers*, p. 13.

The chief present-day mistakes, then, are a lack, on the part of many foundation officials, of this thing called "feel" or "touch," which is a necessity if foundation money is to be more than a dole; and not using funds as venture capital.

Now, what are the chief difficulties the foundations think they face today? Again, the answers to the 1952 Select Committee Questionnaire throw considerable light on the question.

Before presenting a summary of foundation views, however, it may be noted that official opinion varies on the relative difficulty of operating foundations. Apropos of Julius Rosenwald's famous aphorism, that it is easier to make a million dollars than give it away intelligently, Russell C. Leffingwell, chairman of the Board of Trustees of the Carnegie Corporation of New York, thought there was nothing to it. He felt that it was an extraordinarily difficult job to make a million dollars, honestly or otherwise, and he was sure that 150 million other Americans would agree with him. He admitted that it took a lot of hard work to make a successful foundation, but if good men were picked they could and would do the job.[1]

On the other hand, Paul Hoffman, then president of the Ford Foundation, testified that after heading that foundation for two years he was sure that Rosenwald's statement was correct. His explanation was that in business one has a profit and loss gauge that positively indicates success or failure. No such mechanism exists in foundation work, therefore the necessity for painful soul-searching by foundation executives in evaluating their work.[2]

Regardless of the answer to the relative difficulty of business and philanthropic operations, many of the foundations felt that they were confronted by severe problems.[3]

Minor difficulties were: pressure from applicants to contribute to palliative causes; operating in the face of possible government restrictions, particularly those of a monetary or fiscal nature; the difficulty of evaluating completed projects or

[1] *Hearings*, Statement of Russell C. Leffingwell, pp. 370–371.

[2] *Ibid.*, Statement of Paul G. Hoffman, p. 262.

[3] *Questionnaire*, sec. G-3d. See p. 136.

of putting them across to the public as enterprises worthy of public support.

The four main difficulties, however, appeared to be:

1. A scarcity of the gifted or talented, for foundation work, who have that oft-mentioned "feel" or "touch."

A corresponding scarcity of the gifted or talented to whom the foundations could entrust research and other projects. The Milbank Memorial Fund, in short, poignant sentences, expressed this view: "The greatest difficulty is to find the best brains. Qualified workers are comparatively few."[1] The Twentieth Century Fund also stated that this search for superior men formed its principal difficulty. It added, regretfully, that it did not know any recipe for remedying the difficulty.[2]

2. A lack of adequate knowledge concerning the character and quality of the results to be expected from prospective grantees. Apparently this is a paradoxical difficulty. As the venture-capital function is embraced by more foundations, their area of knowledge concerning foreseeable or measurable results decreases. Thus, there is an accentuation of this difficulty at a time when it assumes increasing importance. The Carnegie Endowment for International Peace sums up this viewpoint in these words:

> The principal difficulties faced by foundations in achieving maximum results, aside from limited resources, arise from the inherent obstacles created by inadequate knowledge, changing world conditions and the extraordinary demands upon imagination and foresight implicit in the main role of the foundation today, that of providing venture capital for ideas.[3]

3. Closely allied is the difficulty of choosing from among myriad requests for aid those best suited to the purpose and program of the foundation.

4. Finally, the difficulty of keeping the public sufficiently informed of activities. This was thought to be an increasing problem as the foundations engaged in work of a more venturesome or controversial nature.

[1] Milbank Memorial Fund, *Answers*, p. 36.
[2] Twentieth Century Fund, *Answers*, p. 46.
[3] Carnegie Endowment for International Peace, *Answers*, p. 105.

The comments of the Maurice and Laura Falk Foundation aptly summarized the last three difficulties:

> Their principal difficulties have been (1) always to get adequate and sufficiently reliable information to enable them reasonably to foresee in what respects their pioneering projects are most likely to encounter barriers to success, and (2) to keep the public sufficiently aware of the risk-taking nature of their activities to assure public tolerance of failure when it occurs.[1]

Need for Foundations

Despite testimony that foundation expenditures amounted to only 3 per cent of total philanthropic expenditures in the United States,[2] American foundations have undoubtedly been one of the great social and cultural forces in twentieth-century life, both in the United States and abroad. Hollis ranked them immediately below church, school, and government, as one of the most influential social forces.[3] A cataloguing of all the effects which, directly or indirectly, they have had would certainly give ample proof of this statement. Such a cataloguing is manifestly impossible. Even the foundations, when asked for opinions on the relative effects they might have had in various fields, figuratively threw up their hands in horror.[4] The experienced General Education Board held that the "question is difficult to answer because there is no adequate record of the work of all American foundations." Furthermore, it concluded:

> We are dealing with imponderables. The influence of foundations is closely meshed with a far greater set of influences which derive from the church, the school, the home and all the traditions of our past. To attempt to unravel a single thread from the total skein is probably impossible.[5]

For the most part, in answering these questions, they could merely point to various outstanding projects or programs which they initiated or with which they were connected.

---

[1] Maurice and Laura Falk Foundation, *Answers*, p. 14.

[2] *Hearings*, Statement of F. Emerson Andrews, p. 14.

[3] *Ibid.*, Statement of Ernest V. Hollis, p. 4.

[4] *Questionnaire*, sec. E-3f, h; 4f, h; 5f, 9; 6d, f; sec. G-3a, b. See pp. 133–136.

[5] General Education Board, *Answers*, pp. 112, 114.

Keppel felt that the foundations could "safely rest their case" on these three accomplishments alone: (1) the responsibility of the General Education Board for the improvement of secondary education and education in general in the South; (2) the Rockefeller Foundation program of public health all over the world; and (3) the Carnegie libraries.[1]

Despite their record of accomplishment on relatively meager resources, there has been some conjecturing that the government could and perhaps should take over and assume the foundation role. Since much of the work formerly performed by the foundations has been assumed by government and since many aspects of their work overlap, there is a certain amount of plausibility in the argument. Even Keppel stated:

> As believers in democracy, we are bound to look forward to the day when the community will take over the functions now performed by the foundations of the type we have discussed, and the latter will accordingly disappear or, at any rate, become a factor of relatively slight importance.

He quickly added:

> If we are honest with ourselves, however, we must recognize that that day will not come in our time nor in that of our children or grandchildren.[2]

Even in such fields as the natural sciences, where government support has entered in tremendous proportions, it is felt that the foundations can still play a very important role. For they can provide an *alter ego*, albeit small, that may well open doors which are closed, for one reason or another, to government.[3]

Successive foundation officials, offering testimony to the 1952 House Select Committee, emphasized their belief that it would be unwise to delegate all foundation functions to government. Their opinions were based mainly on the ability of foundations to take risks which, because of political considera-

[1] Keppel, Frederick P., *The Foundation*, pp. 112–113.
[2] *Ibid.*, pp. 110–111.
[3] *Hearings*, Statement of Vannevar Bush, p. 152; Charles Dollard, p. 356.

tions, it would be impossible for the government to take. This was felt to be particularly true in the social science field.[1] Prominent educators expressing views on the subject were of the same opinion.[2]

All of the foundations answering the House Select Committee's Questionnaire believed that the role they played could not be performed effectively by government. They also maintained that, particularly in the social sciences, the government could not be so objective and unbiased as private foundations, nor could it move so swiftly in reaching decisions when promising opportunities presented themselves. Objections were also raised as to the over-all efficiency of government operation in the philanthropic and educational fields.[3] In his reply to the Committee's information-seeking letters, the president of the New York Stock Exchange, a former educator, bluntly stated in this regard that "if the Government begins to stick its finger into the pie, I fear greatly that inevitably red tape, restrictions and lack of freedom will follow."[4]

The foundations also expressed the fear that political considerations would soon become uppermost if the government were to attempt to supplant foundations. Increased taxation was another major objection. Thus, efforts on the part of the government to assume foundation functions "would result in another sprawling bureaucracy with branches spread all over the country or perhaps the world. Experience justifies the statement that another great burden would be imposed on taxpayers."[5]

By far the greatest objection to the replacement of foundations by the government was that such a step would ultimately lead to totalitarianism of one brand or another. A wise people,

[1] *Ibid.*, Statement of Paul G. Hoffman, p. 251; Charles Dollard, p. 352; Russell C. Leffingwell, p. 376; Michael Whitney Straight, p. 421; Marshall Field, pp. 447–448; Raymond B. Fosdick, pp. 759–760.

[2] McBride, Katharine, Solicited Letter to Select Committee, December 3, 1952; Frank H. Sparks, November 14, 1952; William B. Tolley, December 12, 1952.

[3] *Questionnaire*, sec. G-2. See p. 136.

[4] Funston, G. Keith, Solicited Letter to Select Committee, November 26, 1952.

[5] El Pomar Foundation, *Answers to Questionnaire*, p. 25.

it was asserted, should never surrender exclusive rights concerning its welfare to any one institution, least of all to the state. The Max C. Fleischmann Foundation of Nevada asserted:

> The assumption of such functions by the government would be "a" (if not the "last") step towards a totalitarian state. It would destroy the two party system with its opportunity for a change if desired—because control of all these functions would entrench one party beyond the possibility of removal. It would be a compliance with communistic aims and beliefs.[1]

In the light of the belief that foundations are supplying a vital need which cannot be supplied by government, what of their future?

In the past large foundations were the fruit of economic and financial conditions which permitted the accumulation of vast surplus wealth, much of it from current income. Opinion varies as to the number of large foundations that will be created in the future. Some hold that few large foundations will be created in view of the high tax rates and the general tendency toward a wider spread of the wealth.[2]

Differing opinion holds that although today high levels of taxation prevent the current income accumulations of yore, these very tax rates encourage the contribution of substantial sums from current income to philanthropic causes, including foundations that living donors may have created with this in mind. Moreover, present taxation does not affect increases in value in unrealized assets. Owners of businesses, or substantial shares in businesses, can permit those ownerships to appreciate into very large amounts without being affected by taxation. Upon the death of the owner, heavy estate taxes would have to be paid, but in itself this encourages the disposition of large portions of such accumulations to charity, and in several recent examples, foundations of substantial assets have resulted. These special considerations, therefore, prompt a belief that

---

[1] Max C. Fleischmann Foundation of Nevada, *Answers*, p. 14.

[2] Keppel, Frederick P., *The Foundation*, p. 108; *Hearings*, Statement of Alfred P. Sloan, Jr., pp. 456-457.

the first opinion noted above may be mistaken with respect to foundations.

Regardless of the accuracy of either opinion, if it is desirable that further encouragement be given to foundations, such growth can be assured by (1) revision of the tax laws so as to encourage them[1]; and (2) by the large corporations of the United States creating foundations similar to those already in existence. The corporations could easily do this by taking advantage of the 5 per cent deduction for philanthropic purposes allowed them under existing tax laws.[2]

Arguing in favor of this 5 per cent policy, Alfred P. Sloan, Jr., pointed out that many corporation directors favored the plan but hesitated to take the step. They were fearful of being accused by stockholders of diverting corporation funds for purposes far afield from the stockholders' interests. Sloan felt that these fears were groundless and that as time passed, more and more foundations would be created through the 5 per cent deduction.[3] Corporation foundations, however, usually have a serious disadvantage. Whereas the general purpose foundations are more or less perpetual and can engage in long-range planning, those created by corporations have seldom accumulated sizable corpora; their efficiency is consequently impaired. Despite this drawback, F. Emerson Andrews believes that

> . . . if they are given imaginative direction and some freedom to experiment, corporation foundations may become pioneers and pathfinders in corporate giving, finding ways of applying corporate gifts that will bring increased credit to business and larger benefits to communities.[4]

Although the consensus has been that government cannot perform many of the special functions of private foundations,

[1] For examples, see *Hearings*, Statement of Robert M. Hutchins, p. 286; Marshall Field, p. 448.

[2] See Ruml, Beardsley, and Theodore Geiger, editors, *The Manual of Corporate Giving*. National Planning Association, Washington, 1952.

[3] *Hearings*, Statement of Alfred P. Sloan, Jr., p. 458.

[4] Andrews, F. Emerson, *Corporation Giving*. Russell Sage Foundation, New York, 1952, p. 112. Chapter 6 provides a concise account of corporation foundations.

it should be pointed out that one government foundation does exist, and serves usefully in its own special field, the National Science Foundation. Created in 1950, this Foundation has a twofold role. First, it was set up as an additional source of catalytic, venture capital. Second, it is ultimately to be the coordinator or clearinghouse for government-sponsored, government-financed experimental projects. At the present time its grants are concentrated in the natural science field mainly in the form of fellowships and grants-in-aid for outstanding scholars. In the future it could presumably enter other fields as they become less controversial and more amenable to the scientific method.

CONCLUSION

The larger, private American foundations of today are a flowering of the American capitalistic system and they reflect its characteristics in various ways. Although they have antecedents that run far back in the pages of history, they differ from most previous philanthropic institutions. Despite the mystic, religious note that permeated the creation of many foundations, they are secular and predominantly devoted to secular causes.

They sprang into being during a period when government regulation of individuals and institutions was at, probably, the lowest ebb in human history. Their very range and variety of purposes is exemplification of this freedom; similarly, their diversity of operation. In such matters as selecting officers, making investments of their capital, and the manner in which they actually implement their expressed purposes, they have covered the widest possible latitude. Furthermore, they express or imply a belief that such diversity, as is the case with the capitalistic system, is one of the greatest bulwarks to that freedom from which they came and of which they are a part.

The majority of these foundations differ from previous ones in that they have adopted a preventive rather than palliative concept of their function. Rather than adopting the *status quo* attitude of "what has been will always be," they have attempted, with characteristic American drive and push, to get at the very heart of various problems. This pragmatic "Does it work? and if not, let's get rid of it and substitute something better" permeates the foundations and our capitalistic society alike.

The combination of freedom, wide-ranging activities, and venture-capital programs has, however, brought the foundations a problem which did not face those of previous ages. They are, and have been, accused of using their very freedom of action to control or guide individuals, institutions, and the society of which they are a part. The foundations have a partial defense in the care they have given to the maintenance of an air of freedom for their grantees. Probably their most telling one, however, is that in one generation they were accused of directing America to the right; in the next, of directing her to the left. Even if one believes these accusations, it would seem that there need be little fear of organizations subject to such vagaries. The obvious answer, of course, is that neither is true; both arose from a misunderstanding of foundation purposes, policies, and programs.

Partially to correct these misconceptions, and partially as a result of the humanizing and democratizing influences at work in the American capitalistic system itself, the principle of the public trust became recently a significant factor in foundation thinking. This principle, predicated on the first three foundation principles (diversity of operation, preventive venture-capital function, and freedom of action) seeks to preserve them by making the American public more conscious of what foundations are and have been doing. Public reporting, official and voluntary, is expected to achieve this purpose.

What of the future of foundations? This writer believes that they will continue to play a very necessary role in American society. As the 1952 Select Committee states on page 4 of its *Final Report:* "It appears that the present need for foundations is even greater than it has been in the past and that there is great likelihood that the need will prove an increasing one in the future."

APPENDICES

A P P E N D I X   A

Statistical Information Regarding 54 Larger Foundations

BASED ON THEIR ANSWERS TO QUESTIONNAIRE SUBMITTED BY THE 1952 HOUSE SELECT COMMITTEE
TO INVESTIGATE TAX-EXEMPT FOUNDATIONS AND COMPARABLE ORGANIZATIONS

	Legal nature	Place of origin	Date of origin	Principal office	Original endowment	Present endowment[1]	Net worth	Average annual gross income[2]	Total amount of grants[3]	Average annual foreign grants[4]
Altman Foundation	Corporation	New York	1913	New York	$8,553,847	$11,967,029B	$11,967,029	$498,154	$2,345,384	$0
M.D. Anderson Foundation	Trust	Texas	1936	Houston	10,000	22,624,577B	27,228,965	1,231,119	6,300,058[5]	0
Association for the Aid of Crippled Children	Corporation	New York	1900	New York	500	13,173,406B	13,173,406	489,040	541,877[6]	0
Louis D. Beaumont Foundation	Corporation	Ohio	1933	Cleveland	16,816,735	16,816,735B	16,798,897	701,327	4,193,152[7]	0
Buhl Foundation	Trust	Pennsylvania	1927	Pittsburgh	10,951,157	13,351,678B / 14,310,740M	13,351,678	581,291	6,036,153	0
Carnegie Corporation of New York	Corporation	New York	1911	New York	125,000,000	160,896,715B[8]	177,187,884	5,941,119	77,156,159	410,675
Carnegie Endowment for International Peace	Corporation	New York	1910	New York	10,000,000	11,608,174B / 13,739,623M	13,555,691	620,992	2,549,827	36,706
Carnegie Foundation for the Advancement of Teaching	Corporation	New York	1905	New York	10,000,000	10,855,973B / 12,161,044M	12,255,587	492,915	2,451,573	106,071

	Legal nature	Place of origin	Date of origin	Principal office	Original endowment	Present endowment[1]	Net worth	Average annual gross income[2]	Total amount of grants[3]	Average annual foreign grants[4]
Carnegie Institution of Washington	Corporation	Chartered by U.S. Congress	1902	Washington, D. C.	10,000,000	32,966,047B 39,901,580M	48,940,924	2,328,422[9]	1,628,189[10]	23,449
Amon G. Carter Foundation	Corporation	Texas	1945	Fort Worth	8,755,311	12,054,794B	12,784,476	1,733,917[11]	1,498,655[11]	0
China Medical Board, Inc.	Corporation	New York	1928	New York	12,000,000	25,880,005B 30,238,505M	30,199,647	721,167	9,347,377	515,377
Commonwealth Fund	Corporation	New York	1918	New York	9,956,111	81,170,280B 95,450,754M	85,168,614	1,995,578	32,353,189	300,860
Cullen Foundation	Trust	Texas	1947	Houston	10,000	5,290,467B	4,949,879	1,232,217[12]	9,933,900[12]	0
Duke Endowment	Trust	No. Carolina	1924	New York	40,000,000	105,924,743B 131,105,062M	105,924,742	4,913,332	60,337,540[13]	0
El Pomar Foundation	Corporation	Colorado	1937	Colorado Springs	1,393,367	14,687,720B	14,687,946	507,477	4,690,731[14]	0
Maurice and Laura Falk Foundation	Trust	Pennsylvania	1929	Pittsburgh	3,722,050	6,194,325B 11,698,669M	6,420,697	416,683	4,586,690[15]	0
Samuel S. Fels Fund	Corporation	Pennsylvania	1936	Philadelphia	25,000	12,083,074B	10,441,411	247,604	5,052,476	0
Field Foundation	Corporation	New York	1940	New York	605,000	11,916,402B	13,291,029	695,857	3,052,649[16]	0
Max C. Fleischmann Foundation of Nevada	Trust	Nevada	1951	Reno	20,000	9,770,753B	235,569	9,212[17]	10,250[18]	0
Ford Foundation	Corporation	Michigan	1936	New York	25,000	Not stated	502,587,957	29,061,477	64,443,241[18]	2,387,172[18]
General Education Board	Corporation	Chartered by U.S. Congress	1903	New York	10,000,000	3,533,740B 4,945,883M	10,136,656	519,974	59,101,241	0
John Simon Guggenheim Memorial Foundation	Corporation	New York	1925	New York	3,000,000	30,115,781B	30,692,077	1,082,767	7,019,993[20]	91,555
John A. Hartford Foundation	Corporation	New York	1929	New York	25,000	10,000,000[21]	1,513,901	87,975[22]	2,818,288[22]	0
Charles Hayden Foundation	Corporation	New York	1937	New York	44,039,153	47,845,681B 53,927,248M	52,292,865	1,745,877	22,092,636[23]	0
Eugene Higgins Scientific Trust	Trust	New York	1948	New York	Not determined	34,491,321B	34,491,321	1,000,000[22]	2,640,000[24]	0
Louis W. and Maud Hill Family Foundation	Corporation	Minnesota	1934	St. Paul	147,675	12,368,257B	13,538,236	334,330	1,453,469[14]	0
Houston Endowment	Corporation	Texas	1937	Houston	1,794,215	3,082,225	8,606,590	1,622,463	1,441,149[14]	0
Godfrey M. Hyams Trust	Trust	Massachusetts	1921	Boston	10,992,910	10,900,236B 13,703,111M	11,401,431	600,893	7,705,515	0

Statistical Information Regarding 54 Larger Foundations (CONTINUED)

BASED ON THEIR ANSWERS TO QUESTIONNAIRE SUBMITTED BY THE 1952 HOUSE SELECT COMMITTEE TO INVESTIGATE TAX-EXEMPT FOUNDATIONS AND COMPARABLE ORGANIZATIONS

	Legal nature	Place of origin	Date of origin	Principal office	Original endowment	Present endowment[1]	Net worth	Average annual gross income[2]	Total amount of grants[3]	Average annual foreign grants[4]
James Foundation of New York	Corporation	New York	1941	New York	19,734,330	31,275,901B 46,464,383M	31,275,901	2,129,535	12,019,800[16]	0
Juilliard Musical Foundation	Corporation	New York	1920	New York	13,460,508	11,831,628B 13,856,107M	16,673,408	519,038	6,662,697	0
Henry J. Kaiser Family Foundation	Trust	California	1948	Oakland	10,000	14,909,315B	14,962,442	13,146[22]	32,700[25]	0
W. K. Kellogg Foundation	Corporation	Michigan	1930	Battle Creek	21,600,000	33,323,941B 51,000,000M	66,550,323	3,253,337	32,536,405[26]	315,839a
Kresge Foundation	Corporation	Michigan	1924	Detroit	1,357,376	79,313,361B 94,865,923M	85,149,762	4,776,136	18,860,601	0
Kate Macy Ladd Fund	Corporation	New York	1946	Newark, N. J.	10,816,999	11,201,129B 14,080,199M	11,212,082	436,178[11]	Not listed[10]	0
Edward Drummond Libbey Trust	Trust	Ohio	1925	Toledo	15,649,297	15,658,549B	15,707,899	565,038	Not listed[27]	0
Lilly Endowment	Corporation	Indiana	1937	Indianapolis	280,000	27,218,855B 58,307,673M	27,218,855	1,461,820	8,843,325[28]	14,000
Josiah Macy, Jr., Foundation	Corporation	New York	1930	New York	5,018,157	17,736,672B 20,206,852M	18,068,636	377,875	3,089,059[29]	280
John and Mary R. Markle Foundation	Corporation	New York	1927	New York	3,001,980	17,321,102B 21,485,118M	19,026,006	727,811	10,303,916	50,642
Mayo Association	Corporation	Minnesota	1919	Rochester, Minn.	3,200,000	44,536,164B 44,762,138M	44,536,164	2,209,488	8,664,914[14]	0
A.W. Mellon Educational and Charitable Trust	Trust	Pennsylvania	1930	Pittsburgh	10,000	34,202,504B 59,704,678M	34,202,504	1,762,742	92,459,340	0
Milbank Memorial Fund	Corporation	New York	1905	New York	2,958,652	11,678,704B 13,728,652M	11,678,704	601,181	4,048,940	5,611

	Legal nature	Place of origin	Date of origin	Principal office	Original endowment	Present endowment[1]	Net worth	Average annual gross income[2]	Total amount of grants[3]	Average annual foreign grants[4]
William H. Miner Foundation	Trust	Illinois	1923	Chicago	637,840	12,441,015B	12,441,015	1,051,936	4,306,051	0
Charles Stewart Mott Foundation	Corporation	Michigan	1926	Flint	Not ascertained	14,436,935B	14,436,935	420,000	3,168,014	0
William Rockhill Nelson Trust	Trust	Missouri	1926	Kansas City	11,000,000	10,935,182B	12,031,602	632,830	8,275,817[30]	0
New York Foundation	Corporation	New York	1909	New York	100,000	9,634,488B 12,923,157M	10,277,460	465,365	4,876,847[31]	0
Old Dominion Foundation	Corporation	Virginia	1941	New York	3,743,618	18,755,381B	15,981,151	669,251	11,319,943[16]	15,600
Olin Foundation	Corporation	New York	1938	New York	16,000,000[32]	46,000,000B[32]	26,051,006	978,330	3,046,416[5]	0
Rockefeller Foundation	Corporation	New York	1913	New York	100,000,000	137,463,435B 321,954,125M	323,159,078	11,363,589	219,886,042[33]	3,474,544
Rosenberg Foundation	Corporation	California	1935	San Francisco	1,158,006	7,375,981M	6,944,123	196,239	993,376[11]	0
Russell Sage Foundation	Corporation	New York	1907	New York	10,000,000	13,987,556B 16,376,182M	14,258,342	541,760	2,822,514[24]	0
Alfred P. Sloan Foundation	Corporation	Delaware	1934	New York	500,000	29,338,956M	33,836,724	1,265,041	13,800,902	0
Surdna Foundation	Corporation	New York	1917	Yonkers	150,000	18,162,748B	18,162,748	755,621	7,558,348[25]	0
Estate of Harry Trexler	Trust	Pennsylvania	1934	Allentown	9,184,181	12,675,549B	12,675,549	432,992	4,501,516[35]	0
Twentieth Century Fund	Corporation	Massachusetts	1919	New York	417,000	9,879,497B	9,879,497	456,975	Not listed[26]	0

[1] Book or market value is indicated by the letters B and M following the figures. Where available, both values are given.
[2] For 1946–1951 unless otherwise indicated.
[3] For 1935–1951 unless otherwise indicated.
[4] For 1947–1951 unless otherwise indicated.
[5] For 1939–1951.
[6] For 1949–1951; primarily an operating foundation.
[7] For 1945–1951.
[8] Cost or market value, whichever is lower.
[9] Includes net gains from security transactions together with gifts and grants averaging $98,200 per year.
[10] Primarily an operating foundation.
[11] For 1947–1951.

[12] For nine months in 1947 and for 1948–1951.
[13] For 1936–1951.
[14] For 1937–1951.
[15] For 1936–1950.
[16] For 1941–1951.
[17] For 1952.
[18] For 1951.
[19] For 1948–1952.
[20] For 1925–1952.
[21] In excess of this amount.
[22] For 1948–1951.
[23] For 1937–1952.
[24] For 1950–1951.

[25] For 1949–1951.
[26] For 1930–1951.
[27] By terms of will all net income is paid to the Toledo, Ohio, Museum of Art.
[28] For 1938–1951.
[29] For 1930–1949.
[30] For 1926–1951.
[31] For 1936–1949.
[32] After recent revaluation of stock holdings.
[33] Appropriations.
[34] Primarily an operating foundation since 1948.
[35] For 1934–1951.
[36] Primarily an operating foundation since 1937.

Questionnaire Submitted by the Select Committee to the Larger Foundations

Created by House Resolution 561, Eighty-second Congress, Second Session, to Investigate Tax-Exempt Foundations and Comparable Organizations

INSTRUCTIONS

1. Answers to the questionnaire should be made to the committee in duplicate.

2. Answers should be prepared so that they are carefully keyed to the section and question number of each section. No particular form other than reference to section and question number need be observed. However, in order to avoid confusion and expedite processing, it is requested that the answers to each section should begin on a page separate from those on which answers to another section have been given. In other words, when beginning answers to any section please use a sheet of paper on which no other answers have been made.

3. The committee places a higher premium on clarity and substance than on style and form; on speed of completion rather than on niceties of phrase. Write as much or as little as is deemed necessary to answer the questions. The committee wishes your best thinking but will appreciate such brevity and compression as is consonant with clear exposition.

4. Please use one side only of regular 8½ by 11 letter-size paper for your answers, double-spaced and numbered serially at the top irrespective of section, with the name of your organization at the top of each page.

SECTION A

A–1. What is the name of your organization?

A–2. What is its legal nature, i. e., a trust, a corporation, or other type of association?

A–3. If a corporation, in what State is it incorporated and by what State agency?

A-4. Where is its principal office located?

A-5. When was it chartered or otherwise organized?

A-6. Is it the outgrowth or continuation of a form of predecessor organization, or the result of a merger? Explain.

A-7. (*a*) Has it been declared exempt from taxation under section 101 (6) or any other section of the Internal Revenue Code by the Commissioner of Internal Revenue? If so, when was such exemption granted?

(*b*) Has its exemption ever been removed, suspended, or challenged by the Commissioner of Internal Revenue? If so, state when and the circumstances thereof.

A-8. If it is in the nature of a trust, is it permitted deductions for charitable and related contributions as provided by section 162 of the Internal Revenue Code?

A-9. Give the names, addresses (business or mailing) and terms of all trustees or members of your board of directors since 1935.

A-10. Is any of your trustees, members of your board of directors, or executive officers the creator of your organization or a contributor, present or past, to your organization, or a brother or sister (whole or half blood), spouse, ancestor, or lineal descendant of such creator or contributor? If so, explain.

A-11. Is any of your trustees, members of your board of directors, or executive officers also a trustee, director, or officer of any other tax-exempt organization or of any corporation or other business organization related directly or indirectly to your organization? If so, explain in detail.

A-12. List the names and addresses of the principal executive officers of your organization.

A-13. What was the amount of your original endowment and in what manner was it granted to your organization?

A-14. What capital additions over $10,000 in amount have you received since your original endowment and from what sources?

A-15. Is your endowment fund perpetual or is it expendable on an optional or determined liquidating basis? Explain.

A-16. What is the amount of your present endowment?

A-17. Attach a balance sheet indicating the amounts of your assets, liabilities, and net worth as of the close of your last fiscal year.

A-18. What was your average gross income for the years 1946-51, both years inclusive?

SECTION B

B-1. What is the purpose or purposes for which your organization was created as defined by your charter or other instrument creating your organization?

B–2. State the activities which your organization considers permissible under the purpose or purposes stated in your answer to question 1.

B–3. Who determines whether the funds of your organization are being spent within the limitations set forth in your answers to questions 1 and 2?

B–4. Who determines what gifts, grants, loans, contributions, or expenditures are to be made by your organization?

B–5. On what are the determinations specified in question 4 based?

B–6. With whom do proposals submitted to the person, persons, or group named in your answer to question 4 for gifts, grants, loans, contributions, and expenditures originate?

B–7. Is any individual or group of individuals charged with the duty of originating and developing plans, programs, and proposals for the distribution of your funds?

B–8. If the answer to question 7 is in the affirmative, state the names and positions of such persons.

B–9. Was an investigation of each individual named or specified in your answers to questions 3, 4, 7, and 8 made into his or her background and qualifications before he or she was elected, appointed, employed, or otherwise entrusted with his or her duties or responsibilities?

B–10. If the answer to question 9 is in the affirmative, give details as to the nature of such investigations, the manner in which they were conducted, and by whom.

B–11. If the answer to question 9 is in the affirmative, state when such investigations were first instituted.

B–12. If the answer to question 9 is in the affirmative, state the reasons for making such investigations, whether there has been any change in the policy of your organization in relation thereto, and, if so, the date and reasons therefor.

B–13. If the answer to question 9 is in the affirmative, state whether the results of such investigations were reduced to writing or if any memoranda were made in connection therewith.

B–14. If the answer to question 13 is in the affirmative, state whether such writings or memoranda (a) were extant as of January 1951, (b) are extant now, and (c) if extant, the person, firm, corporation, or organization in whose possession or custody they are.

B–15. If the answer to question 9 is in the affirmative, state whether any such investigation revealed any person hired or employed by or affiliated with your organization who at the time of the investigation had or prior thereto had had any affiliations with communist-front organizations.

B-16. If the answer to question 15 is in the affirmative, state the name or names of such person or persons.

B-17. If the answer to question 9 is in the negative, state whether such investigations were ever considered or discussed by your organization or the trustees, board of directors, or officers thereof, and, if so, by whom, and the basis of any decision reached in connection therewith.

B-18. If the answer to question 15 is in the affirmative, state what action was taken by your organization with reference to such person or persons.

B-19. What steps, if any, have been or are being taken to prevent infiltration of your organization by subversive persons?

B-20. If the answer to question 19 is in the negative, state whether you think it necessary or advisable to initiate procedures to prevent possible infiltration of subversives into your organization; and, if so, whether you intend to do so and the general routine of the intended procedures.

SECTION C

C-1. Have any gifts, grants, loans, contributions, or expenditures been made by your organization which were not in accordance with the purpose or purposes defined by the instrument establishing or creating your organization or the permissible activities of your organization set forth in your answers to questions 1 and 2 of section B?

C-2. If the answer to question 1 is in the affirmative, list the amount, recipient, date, and nature of such gift, grant, loan, contribution, or expenditure.

C-3. Does your organization follow up gifts, grants, loans, or contributions made by it to other foundations, agencies, institutions, or groups by investigation to determine the ultimate disposition of such moneys?

C-4. Has any gift, grant, loan, or contribution been made by you to another foundation, agency, organization, institution, or group which in turn made or makes gifts, grants, loans, contributions, or expenditures which are not permissible under your charter or instrument establishing your organization?

C-5. If the answer to question 4 is in the affirmative, list the amount, recipient, date, and nature of each such gift, grant, loan, contribution, or expenditure and the reasons for the making thereof.

C-6. In the making of gifts, grants, loans, contributions, or other expenditures does your organization consult with any other organizations such as the United States Government, educational groups, religious groups, labor groups, veterans' societies, patriotic societies, foreign governments, other foreign agencies? If so, explain.

C–7. List those institutions, operating agencies, publications, specific projects, and individuals which have received aid from your organization and the amounts and years and nature of such aid since 1935. (NOTE.—(a) If your filing system is so set up, it is desired that the lists be made up in alphabetical order. (b) Lists that are included as sections of published works will be accepted in fulfillment of 7 above.)

SECTION D

D–1. State your definition and your understanding of the meaning of the term "subversive" as that term is commonly used in public print today as applied to the activities of an individual, individuals, groups of individuals, an organization, or an institution in relation to the government of the United States.

D–2. Does your organization make any attempt to determine whether the immediate or eventual recipient (whether an individual, group of individuals, association, institution, or organization) of any grant, gift, loan, contribution, or expenditure made by your organization has been or is "subversive" as you have defined that term in answer to question 1, in advance of and/or after making such grant, gift, loan, contribution, or expenditure?

D–3. If the answer to question 2 is in the affirmative, state the nature of such attempted determination, how made, by whom, whether the results thereof are reduced to writing, and, if so, whether they are extant and where?

D–4. If the answer to question 2 is in the affirmative, state when such attempts were first initiated and why; also state whether such attempts have been made sporadically or whether such is established policy, and if the latter, when such policy was established.

D–5. If the answer to question 2 is in the negative, state whether such attempts were ever considered or discussed by your organization, its trustees, directors, or officers, and if so, by whom and the basis of any decision reached in connection therewith.

D–6. Does your organization check immediate, intermediary, or eventual recipients of grants, gifts, loans, or contributions from your organization against the list of subversive and related organizations prepared by the Attorney General of the United States?*

D–7. If your answer to question 6 is in the affirmative, state whether such listing of an organization by the Attorney General of the United States influences you in the making or withholding of

* List of organizations designated by the Attorney General as within Executive Order No. 9835 according to the classification of Section 3, Part III, of the Executive Order.

grants, gifts, loans, contributions, or expenditures either directly or indirectly to organizations so listed.

D–8. If your answer to question 6 is in the negative, state the reasons therefor fully.

D–9. Do you consider it your duty or responsibility to consider the possible effects of grants, gifts, loans, or contributions to organizations which have been so listed by the Attorney General of the United States?

D–10. Has your organization made any grants, gifts, loans, contributions, or expenditures either directly or indirectly through other organizations to any organization so listed by the Attorney General of the United States or to any individual, individuals, or organizations considered "subversive" as you have defined that term in answer to question 1?

D–11. If your answer to question 10 is in the affirmative, list the recipient and date of each such grant, gift, loan, contribution, or expenditure and the amount and nature thereof.

D–12. If your answer to question 10 is in the affirmative, state whether you knew such organization had been so listed by the Attorney General or was considered "subversive" at the time you made such grant, gift, loan, contribution, or expenditure.

D–13. If your answers to questions 10 and 12 are both in the affirmative, state your reasons for making such grant, gift, loan, contribution, or expenditure.

D–14. Has your organization made any grant, gift, loan, contribution, or expenditure directly or indirectly to any individual, individuals, group, organization, or institution which grant, gift, loan, contribution, or expenditure or recipient has been criticized or cited by the Un-American Activities Committee of the United States House of Representatives or the Subcommittee on Internal Security of the Judiciary Committee of the United States Senate?

D–15. If your answer to question 14 is in the affirmative, list the recipient and date of each such grant, gift, loan, contribution, or expenditure and the amount and nature thereof.

D–16. Does your organization consult the "Guide to Subversive Organizations and Publications," House Document No. 137, prepared and released by the Committee on Un-American Activities, United States House of Representatives? If so, for what purpose and to what effect?

SECTION E

E–1. In your opinion, should educational and philanthropic foundations and other comparable organizations which are exempt from Federal income taxation finance or sponsor projects which may have as a direct result the influencing of public opinion in the fields of politics? Economics? Education? International relations? Religion? Government and Public Administration? Other Fields? Explain fully.

E–2. In your opinion, should a tax-exempt foundation which makes a grant to an individual, a group, institution, or organization:

(a) Indicate the conclusions to be reached?

(b) Withdraw its grant or discontinue it if conclusions different from those held by the foundation are reached?

(c) Suppress the findings if they differ from the views of the foundation? Explain fully.

E–3. Explain in detail the activities, if any, of your organization in the field of education both within and outside the territorial limits of the United States. The following questions should be covered fully, but your answer need not be limited thereto:

(a) What policies govern your activities in this field, and who formulates said policies?

(b) Do you consult individuals or groups other than those employed or otherwise directly connected with your organization in the formulation of policies in this field? Explain.

(c) Is an effort made to aid, assist, or support individuals, groups, or projects representing divergent views on controversial educational issues? If so, explain how this is accomplished. If not, explain the reasons therefor.

(d) Is any assistance provided by you for projects in this field conducted by religious or sectarian educational groups, associations, schools, colleges, or universities? If so, is an effort made to secure an equal distribution of moneys among the various major religious groups or sects? If such an effort is not made, why is it not made?

(e) With whom do you consult with regard to financing educational projects outside the territorial limits of the United States? Do you consult with any United States Government agencies, including the United States State Department?

(f) In your opinion, what effect, if any, has your organization had on education in the United States? In other countries?

(g) Does your organization directly or indirectly sponsor or otherwise support proposed or pending State or Federal legislation within the United States or legislation in foreign countries in the field of education? Explain.

(h) In your opinion, what effect have educational and philanthropic foundations and comparable organizations had on education in the United States? In other countries?

E–4. Explain in detail the activities of your organization in the field of international relations both within and outside the territorial limits of the United States. The following questions should be covered fully, but your answer need not be limited thereto:

(a) What policies govern your activities in this field and who formulates said policies?

(b) Do you consult individuals or groups other than those employed or otherwise directly connected with your organization in the formulation of your policies in this field? Explain fully.

(c) Is an effort made to aid, assist, or support individuals, groups, or projects representing divergent views on controversial international issues? If so, explain how this is accomplished. If not, explain the reasons therefor.

(d) Explain in detail the relationship your organization has had with the League of Nations and the United Nations or any of its related agencies.

(e) Explain in detail your relationship with the State Department and any other Government agencies in this field.

(f) In your opinion, what effect, if any, has your organization had on the foreign policies of the United States? On the policies of the United Nations? On the policies of other nations?

(g) Does your organization directly or indirectly sponsor or support any proposed or pending State or Federal legislation or legislation in foreign countries in the field of international relations?

(h) In your opinion, what effect, if any, have educational and philanthropic foundations and comparable organizations had on international relations? On the foreign policies of the United States? On the policies of the United Nations? On the policies of other nations?

E–5. Explain in detail the activities of your organization in the field of government and public administration. The following questions should be answered fully, but your answer need not be limited thereto:

(a) What policies govern your activities in this field, and who formulates said policies?

(b) Do you consult individuals or groups other than those employed or otherwise directly connected with your organization in the formulation of your policies in this field? Explain fully.

(c) Is an effort made to aid, assist, or support individuals, groups, or projects representing divergent views on controversial governmental and public administration issues? If so, explain how this is accomplished. If not, explain the reasons therefor.

(d) Explain in detail your relationship with United States Government agencies in this field.

(e) Does your organization directly or indirectly sponsor or support pending or proposed State, Federal, or foreign legislation in this field? Explain.

(*f*) In your opinion, what effect has your organization had on governmental and public administration matters in the United States? In other countries?

(*g*) In your opinion, what effect have educational and philanthropic foundations and comparable organizations had on governmental and public administration matters in the United States? In other countries?

E-6. Explain in detail the activities of your organization in the field of economics. The following questions should be answered fully, but your answer need not be limited thereto:

(*a*) What policies govern your activities in this field, and who formulates said policies?

(*b*) Do you consult individuals or groups other than those employed or otherwise directly connected with your organization in the formulation of policies in this field? Explain fully.

(*c*) Is an effort made to aid, assist, or support individuals, groups, or projects representing divergent views on controversial economic issues? If so, explain how this is accomplished. If not, explain the reasons therefor.

(*d*) In your opinion, what effect has your organization had on the economic life of the United States?

(*e*) Does your organization directly or indirectly sponsor or otherwise support proposed or pending State or Federal legislation in the field of economics? Explain.

(*f*) In your opinion, what effect have educational and philanthropic foundations and comparable organizations had on the economic life of the United States?

E-7. (*a*) Has your organization ever contributed any funds to any individual, individuals, group, or organization within or without the United States for political purposes? Explain.

(*b*) Has your organization ever contributed any funds to any individual, individuals, group, or organization for nonpolitical purposes, which funds were nevertheless actually used for political purposes? Explain.

SECTION F

F-1. Is your organization engaged in any activities in foreign countries other than those which you have indicated in your answers to prior sections of this questionnaire? Explain fully.

F-2. Does your organization maintain offices or agents in any foreign country?

F-3. If your answer to question 2 is in the affirmative, explain fully, giving the number of agents in each country who are employees, the nature of their duties, the amounts which they are paid and by whom.

F–4. Does your organization promote activities in any foreign country through any foreign organizations or foreign individuals not in your employ? Explain fully.

F–5. If you are engaged in any activities in foreign countries, state the amount of your average annual total budget for such activities during the past 5 years, and give the proportion of such budget to the total amount expended by you during the same period in the United States.

F–6. Does your organization deal directly with the governments of foreign countries in which funds are spent or activity is promoted? Do you deal with any particular political party or group in said countries? Explain fully.

F–7. Is any agent, employee, or affiliate of your organization engaged in political activities in any foreign country? If so, explain fully.

F–8. If your organization is engaged in any activity in foreign countries, do you consult with reference thereto with the United States Department of State? Explain fully.

SECTION G

G–1. What, in your opinion, is the function of tax-exempt philanthropic and educational foundations in society today? Are they supplying a vital need? If so, to what extent?

G–2. In your opinion, could the functions of foundations be effectively performed by government? Explain your answer fully.

G–3. State as succinctly as possible your views on the following:

(a) What contributions to society have foundations made to date?

(b) Have they succeeded in making the maximum use of their potentialities?

(c) What mistakes, if any, have they made?

(d) What are the principal difficulties they face in achieving maximum results?

G–4. In your opinion, has the public a direct interest in tax-exempt foundations and comparable organizations? State the reasons for your answer fully.

G–5. In your opinion, is some form of governmental regulation of foundations necessary or desirable?

G–6. If your answer to question 5 is in the affirmative, give your reasons therefor and state the form such regulation should take.

G–7. If your answer to question 5 is in the negative, give the reasons for your view.

G–8. Do you believe that the charters or other instruments creating educational and philanthropic foundations and comparable organizations should specifically describe the type of activity in which the foundation will engage? Or do you feel it is sufficient to indicate the organization's purpose in general terms as "promotion of human welfare," "diffusion of knowledge," "betterment of mankind"? Explain.

G–9. Do you feel that any limits should be placed on educational and philanthropic foundations and comparable organizations as to the size of endowment, legal life, right of trustees to spend its capital funds, etc.?

SECTION H

H–1. If you have any views or suggestions concerning educational and philanthropic foundations which you have not covered elsewhere in your answers to this questionnaire, the committee will welcome them.

SECTION I

I–1. Name and identify those persons, firms, or organizations, both within and outside your organization, which have had responsibility for preparing the answers to this questionnaire.

I–2. State whether you have consulted with the representatives of other foundations with reference to this questionnaire and the answers thereto after receipt of this questionnaire.

I–3. If your answer to question 2 is in the affirmative, give the names, addresses, and titles of those persons with whom you have consulted.

I–4. State whom, if anyone, you have consulted with reference to this questionnaire in any branch, department, or agency of the United States Government other than the representatives of the Select Committee submitting this questionnaire. Give the names and titles of such individuals.

Bibliography

ALLEN, WILLIAM H., *Modern Philanthropy*. Dodd, Mead and Co., New York, 1912.

ANDREWS, F. EMERSON, *Corporation Giving*. Russell Sage Foundation, New York, 1952.

————, *Philanthropic Giving*. Russell Sage Foundation, New York, 1950.

————, "Philanthropy's Venture Capital," *Educational Record*, vol. 32, October, 1951, pp. 361–370.

AYRES, LEONARD P., *Seven Great Foundations*. Russell Sage Foundation, New York, 1911.

BURNS, ALLEN T., "The Place of Philanthropic Foundations in a Community," *Proceedings of the National Conference of Social Work*, 1919, pp. 676–678.

CANDLER, WARREN A., *Dangerous Donations and Degrading Doles*, or A Vast Scheme for Capturing and Controlling the Colleges and Universities of the Country. Privately printed, Atlanta, Ga. (?), 1909.

CANNON, CORNELIA J., "Philanthropic Doubts," *Atlantic Monthly*, vol. 128, September, 1921, pp. 289–293.

CARNEGIE, ANDREW, *The Gospel of Wealth and Other Timely Essays*. Doubleday, Doran and Co., Garden City, N. Y., 1933.

————, *Triumphant Democracy:* Fifty Years' March of the Republic. Doubleday, Doran and Co., Garden City, N. Y., 1933.

CARNEGIE CORPORATION OF NEW YORK, *Annual Reports*. The Corporation, 1922–.

CARNEGIE FOUNDATION FOR THE ADVANCEMENT OF TEACHING, *Annual Reports*. The Foundation, New York, 1906–.

CARNEGIE INSTITUTION OF WASHINGTON, *Yearbooks*. The Institution, Washington, 1902–.

COFFMAN, HAROLD C., *American Foundations:* A Study of Their Role in the Child Welfare Movement. Association Press, New York, 1936.

COMMONWEALTH FUND, *Annual Reports*. The Fund, New York, 1919–.

COON, HORACE, *Money to Burn:* What the Great American Philanthropic Foundations Do with Their Money. Longmans, Green and Co., New York, 1938.

DEVINE, EDWARD T., "The Dominant Note of the Modern Philanthropy," *Proceedings of the National Conference of Charities and Correction*, 1906, pp. 1–10.

DODGE, FAITH HUNTER, "In the Service of Humanity," *Pan-American Magazine*, vol. 41, December, 1928, pp. 198–204.

EATON, BERRIEN C., JR., "Charitable Foundations, Tax Avoidance and Business Expediency," *Virginia Law Review*, vol. 35, November, 1949, pp. 809–861; December, 1949, pp. 987–1051.

EMBREE, EDWIN R., "The Business of Giving Away Money," *Harper's Magazine*, vol. 161, August, 1930, pp. 320–329; "Timid Billions: Are the Foundations Doing Their Job?" *Ibid.*, vol. 198, March, 1949, pp. 28–37.

—— and JULIA WAXMAN, *Investment in People:* The Story of the Julius Rosenwald Fund. Harper and Bros., New York, 1949.

FALK FOUNDATION, MAURICE and LAURA, *Reports*. The Foundation, Pittsburgh, 1933–.

FIELD FOUNDATION, *Annual Reports*. The Foundation, New York, 1949–.

FLEXNER, ABRAHAM, *Funds and Foundations*. Harper and Bros., New York, 1952.

——, *Medical Education in the United States and Canada:* A Report to the Carnegie Foundation for the Advancement of Teaching. Bulletin 4. The Foundation, New York, 1910.

——, "Private Fortunes and the Public Future," *Atlantic Monthly*, vol. 156, August, 1935, pp. 215–224.

FORD FOUNDATION, *Report of the Study for the Ford Foundation on Policy and Program*. The Foundation, Detroit, 1949.

FOSDICK, RAYMOND B., *The Story of the Rockefeller Foundation*. Harper and Bros., New York, 1952.

FUND FOR THE ADVANCEMENT OF EDUCATION, *Annual Report*. The Fund, New York, 1952.

GENERAL EDUCATION BOARD, *Reports*. The Board, New York, 1902–.

GLENN, JOHN M., LILIAN BRANDT, and F. EMERSON ANDREWS, *Russell Sage Foundation, 1907–1946*. Russell Sage Foundation, New York, 1947.

GOLDTHORPE, J. HAROLD, *Higher Education, Philanthropy, and Federal Tax Exemption*, edited by Dorothy Leemon. Series V, no. 7, American Council on Education Studies. The Council, Washington, 1944.

GRAY, B. KIRKMAN, *Philanthropy and the State*, or Social Politics. P. S. King and Co., London, 1908.

HARRISON, SHELBY M., and F. EMERSON ANDREWS, *American Foundations for Social Welfare*. Russell Sage Foundation, New York, 1946.

HOLLIS, ERNEST V., "Evolution of the Philanthropic Foundation," *Educational Record*, vol. 20, October, 1939, pp. 575–588.

———, *Philanthropic Foundations and Higher Education*. Columbia University Press, New York, 1938.

HURLIN, RALPH G., "Trends Shown in the Establishment of Recent Foundations," *Changing Conditions in Public Giving*, edited by Alfred Williams Anthony. Abbott Press and Mortimer-Walling, Inc., New York, 1929.

JENKINS, EDWARD C., *Philanthropy in America*. Association Press, New York, 1950.

KEPPEL, APPRECIATIONS OF FREDERICK PAUL by Some of His Friends. Columbia University Press, New York, 1951.

KEPPEL, FREDERICK P., "Opportunities and Dangers of Educational Foundations," *School and Society*, vol. 22, December 26, 1925, pp. 793–799.

———, *Philanthropy and Learning*. Columbia University Press, New York, 1936.

———, *The Foundation:* Its Place in American Life. Macmillan Co., New York, 1930.

KOPETZKY, SAMUEL J., *Foundations and Their Trends:* Address Delivered Before the Medical Society of the County of New York, February 23, 1931. Privately printed, New York, 1931.

LASKI, HAROLD, *The Dangers of Obedience and Other Essays*. Harper and Bros., New York, 1930.

LASSER, J. K., "Why Do So Many Business Men Start Foundations?" *Dun's Review*, vol. 57, February, 1949, pp. 15–17, 35–44.

LEAVELL, ULLIN W., *Philanthropy in Negro Education*. George Peabody College for Teachers, Nashville, Tenn., 1930.

LESTER, ROBERT M., *Forty Years of Carnegie Giving*. Charles Scribner's Sons, New York, 1941.

———, "The Philanthropic Endowment in Modern Life," *South Atlantic Quarterly*, vol. 34, January, 1935, pp. 1–14.

LILLY ENDOWMENT, *Annual Reports*. The Endowment, Indianapolis, 1950–.

LINDEMAN, EDUARD C., *Wealth and Culture*. Harcourt, Brace and Co., New York, 1936.

MACY FOUNDATION, JOSIAH, JR., *Reports*. The Foundation, New York, 1932–.

MARKLE FOUNDATION, JOHN and MARY R., *Annual Reports*. The Foundation, New York, 1935–.

MELLON EDUCATIONAL AND CHARITABLE TRUST, A. W., *Reports*. The Trust, Pittsburgh, 1930–.

MILBANK MEMORIAL FUND, *Reports*. The Fund, New York, 1922–.

NEW YORK FOUNDATION, *Report*. The Foundation, New York, 1949.

OGG, FREDERIC A., *Research in the Humanistic and Social Sciences*. Century Co., New York, 1928.

ORTON, WILLIAM A., "Endowments and Foundations," *Encyclopaedia of the Social Sciences*, vol. 5, 1931.

PRITCHETT, HENRY S., "The Use and Abuse of Endowments," *Atlantic Monthly*, vol. 144, October, 1929, pp. 517–524.

RICH, WILMER SHIELDS, and NEVA R. DEARDORFF, editors, *American Foundations and Their Fields*. 6th ed. Raymond Rich Associates, New York, 1948.

ROCKEFELLER FOUNDATION, *Annual Reports*. The Foundation, New York, 1913–.

ROCKEFELLER, JOHN D., "Some Random Reminiscences of Men and Events," *The World's Work*, vol. 17, January, 1909, pp. 11101–11110.

ROCKEFELLER, LAURA SPELMAN, MEMORIAL, *Final Report*. The Memorial, New York, 1933.

ROSENBERG FOUNDATION, *Report*. The Foundation, San Francisco, 1946.

ROSENWALD, JULIUS, "Principles of Public Giving," *Atlantic Monthly*, vol. 143, May, 1929, pp. 599–606; "The Trends Away from Perpetuities," *Ibid.*, vol. 146, December, 1930, pp. 741–749.

RUML, BEARDSLEY, and THEODORE GEIGER, editors, *The Manual of Corporate Giving*. National Planning Association, Washington, 1952.

RUSSELL SAGE FOUNDATION, *Annual Reports*. The Foundation, New York, 1948–.

SLOAN FOUNDATION, ALFRED P., *Reports*. The Foundation, New York, 1951–.

SPELMAN FUND, *Annual Reports*. The Fund, New York, 1921–1936.

TAYLOR, ELEANOR K., *Public Accountability of Foundations and Charitable Trusts*. Russell Sage Foundation, New York, 1953.

"THE MODERN PHILANTHROPIC FOUNDATION: A Critique and a Proposal," *Yale Law Journal*, vol. 59, February, 1950, pp. 477–509.

TWENTIETH CENTURY FUND, *Annual Reports*. The Fund, New York, 1930–.

U.S. CONGRESS, HOUSE OF REPRESENTATIVES. Select Committee to Investigate Tax-Exempt Foundations and Comparable Organizations. *Answers to Questionnaires Submitted to the Larger Foundations*. File Clerk's Office, House of Representatives, Washington, 1952. Unpublished.

————, *Final Report of the Select Committee to Investigate Foundations and Other Organizations*. House Report 2514. 82d Congress, 2d Sess. Government Printing Office, Washington, 1953.

————, *Hearings Before the Select Committee to Investigate Tax-Exempt Foundations and Comparable Organizations*. 82d Congress, 2d Sess. Government Printing Office, Washington, 1953.

————, *Letters from Various Individuals Solicited by the Select Committee to Investigate Tax-Exempt Foundations and Comparable Organizations*. File Clerk's Office, House of Representatives, Washington, 1952. Unpublished.

U.S. CONGRESS, SENATE. Commission on Industrial Relations. *Final Report and Testimony of the Commission on Industrial Relations*. Senate Document 415. 64th Congress, 1st Sess. Government Printing Office, Washington, 1916.

YOUNG, JAMES C., "The Dead Hand in Philanthropy," *Current History*, vol. 23, March, 1936, pp. 837–842.

ZINSSER, HANS, *In Defense of Scholarship:* Address Before the Graduate School of Brown University, Commencement 1929. The University, Providence, 1929.

————, "The Perils of Magnanimity: A Problem in American Education," *Atlantic Monthly*, vol. 139, February, 1927, pp. 246–250.

INDEX

Index

ACCOUNTABILITY, public, of foundations, 101–105
Accumulation, in foundations, 27–28, 109, 122–125
Acts, legislative. *See* Legislation
Agriculture, 39, 52, 60
Aldrich, Malcolm Pratt, 34n, 35n, 100n
Allen, William H., 46n, 86n
Altman Foundation, 30n, 122
American Baptist Educational Society, 21
American Council of Learned Societies, 57, 60
American Council on Education, 7
American Foundations (Coffman), 23n, 28n, 29n, 33n, 56n, 89n, 98n, 108n
American Foundations and Their Fields (4th ed., Seybold; 6th ed., Rich and Deardorff), 61n, 141
American Foundations for Social Welfare (Harrison and Andrews), 22n, 24n, 43n, 61n
Anderson Foundation, M.D., 79n, 122
Andrews, F. Emerson, 7, 11, 12, 21n, 22n, 24n, 26n, 28n, 43, 51n, 52n, 61n, 78n, 81n, 100n, 113n, 117
Annual reports, 12, 81, 89–90, 97, 99–101, 104. *See also* Bibliography; Foundations by name; Reporting, public
Answers to Questionnaire. Submitted to the Larger Foundations by the Select Committee to Investigate Tax-Exempt Foundations and Comparable Organizations, 10, 12
Anthony, Alfred W., 28n, 46n
Appreciations of Frederick Paul Keppel by Some of His Friends, 106n
"Are the Foundations Doing Their Job?" (Embree), 109n
Area programs, 71, 72
Arizona, 34
Arkansas experiment, 65
Arts, fine, 32, 42
Assets, foundation, 12, 122–125
Association for the Aid of Crippled Children, 31n, 122
Atomic bomb, 60
Ayres, Leonard P., 20n

BANTING, Frederick, 109
Barnard, Chester I., 100
Barnard College, 38
Basic research, 54, 63
Beaumont Foundation, Louis D., 122
Bibliography, 139–142
Birmingham-Southern College, 7
Boston (Mass.), 30
Brandt, Lilian, 21n, 81n
Brown University, 95
Buhl Foundation, 49n, 83, 122
Bureau of Internal Revenue, 69, 100
Bureaucracy, 70, 91, 108, 115
Burns, Allen T., 81n
Bush, Vannevar, 19n, 78, 94n, 95, 100n, 114n
"Business of Giving Away Money, The" (Embree), 23n, 61n, 91n
Business operations, 31–44, 70–72, 122–125
Buttrick, Wallace, 21

CALIFORNIA, state of, 34, 75
California, University of, 60
Candler, Bishop Warren A., 74, 75
Cannon, Cornelia J., 47, 89
Canterbury Tales (Chaucer), 17
Capitalism, 23, 25, 92, 94, 95–96, 118, 119
Carnegie, Andrew, 21, 22, 87n
Carnegie Corporation of New York: *Answers to Questionnaire*, 38n, 103n, 110n; creation of, 22; effect of, 114; investments of, 43, 44; officers of, 35; program of, 40, 55, 57, 58, 60, 70, 72, 75; reports of, 12, 28n, 33, 36n, 38, 41n, 44, 47n, 57, 76, 81n, 90n, 91n, 97; statistical information regarding, 122; trustees of, 34, 111; venture-capital concept of, 60; views on the mistakes of foundations, 110; views on the public accountability of foundations, 102, 103
Carnegie Endowment for International Peace, 30n, 72, 80, 112, 122
Carnegie Foundation for the Advancement of Teaching, 26, 49, 51, 63, 74, 122

Carnegie Institution of Washington, 26, 78, 95, 123
Carnegie libraries, 114
Carter Foundation, Amon G., 123
Changing Conditions in Public Giving (Anthony), 28n, 46n
"Charitable Foundations, Tax Avoidance and Business Expediency" (Eaton), 24n
Charitable trusts, 5, 26, 68
Charters and deeds of trust, 26–31, 70, 87, 88, 109
Chaucer, Geoffrey, 17
China Medical Board, Inc., 123
Church, influence of the, in Tudor England, 17–19, 27
Civil War, 19, 20, 21, 63
Coffman, Harold C., 23n, 28n, 29n, 33n, 56n, 89, 98n, 108, 109
Colorado, 29
Colorado Fuel and Iron Company, 85
Columbia University, 71
Commonwealth Fund, 22, 101, 109, 110n, 123
Communism, 91, 96, 116
Community trusts, 11, 108
Concentration of effort, 47
"Conditional granting," 39
Congressional investigations of foundations, 6, 7, 85–88, 92–97, 99, 127
Constantine, Emperor, 16
Consultation, as part of foundation programming, 56–57, 60, 64, 70, 72–73, 93
Control: of foundations, 16–19, 48, 67–70, 88, 102–105; of grantees, 64–66, 74–80
Controversial fields, 39, 52, 53, 64, 90–91, 93, 110, 112
Coon, Horace, 43n
Corporation foundations, 11, 117
Corporation Giving (Andrews), 117n
Corpus Juris Civilis, 16
Couzens Fund, 27
Cox, E. E., 7, 13, 78, 92
Creation of foundations, 19–25
Criticism: 53, 87, 92, 99, 106–113
Cullen Foundation, 30n, 123
Cyclotron, and the atomic bomb, 60

DANGER of obsolescence, 27, 30, 31
Dangerous Donations and Degrading Doles (Candler), 74, 75n
Dangers of Obedience and Other Essays, The (Laski), 107n
"Dead hand," 31
Deardorff, Neva R., 141
Deeds of trust, 26–31
Devine, Edward T., 46n

Diversity of operation, 26–44, 104, 105, 118, 119
Dodge, Faith Hunter, 51n
Dollard, Charles, 32n, 34n, 35n, 36, 40, 41, 43, 53, 54, 94n, 101n, 106n, 109n, 114n, 115n
"Dominant Note of the Modern Philanthropy, The" (Devine), 46n
Donors, 15, 20–23, 26, 88
Duke Endowment, 27, 34, 123

EATON, Berrien C., Jr., 24n
Economics: determinism, 62; fear of foundation control of, 75, 86; foundation support of, 82, 85, 93, 94; interpretation of, 91, 95
Education: fear of foundation control of, 74, 75, 82, 86, 87, 88; foundation support of, 49, 59–66, 102, 108; function of, 50; general, 61, 114; government operations in, 115; process of, 62, 63; progressive, 65, 66, 89; secondary, 114
Eliot, Charles W., 87n
Elizabeth I, Queen, 18
El Pomar Foundation, 104, 115n, 123
Embree, Edwin R., 23, 27n, 33n, 42n, 58n, 61n, 90, 91n, 108, 109n
Endowments, statistical information on, 122–125
"Endowments and Foundations" (Orton), 16n
England, 17–19, 46, 95
Eurich, Alvin C., 65n
"Evolution of the Philanthropic Foundation" (Hollis), 15

FALK Foundation, Maurice and Laura, 28n, 58, 113, 123
Family foundations, 11
Fellowship foundations, 38, 40, 107
Fellowships, 38, 41, 54, 96, 118
Fels Fund, Samuel S., 30n, 123
Field, Marshall, 34n, 35n, 39n, 51n, 78n, 100n, 115n, 117n
Field Foundation, 81n, 123
Final Report of the Select Committee to Investigate Foundations and Other Organizations, 92, 95, 96, 97, 101n, 119
Fine arts, 32, 42
Fleischmann Foundation, Max, 31n, 116, 123
Flexner, Abraham, 21, 48n, 58, 60, 91n, 109
Follow-up procedure: by foundations, concerning grants, 76–78; by government concerning filing of foundation reports, 99

Forand, Aime J., 37
Ford Foundation: officers of, 35, 65, 111; outside consultation of, 73; program of, 58, 59, 65, 70, 72; statistical information regarding, 123; trustees of, 53, 105; venture-capital concept of, 53
Ford, Henry, II, 35n, 53
Foreign activities of foundations. *See* Foundations, foreign activities of
Form 990A, 104
Forty Years of Carnegie Giving (Lester), 22n
Fosdick, Raymond B., 21n, 39, 47n, 63n, 90, 115n
Foundation, The (Keppel), 9n, 19, 21, 22n, 24n, 30n, 32n, 35n, 36n, 41n, 42n, 45n, 51n, 52n, 55n, 57n, 63n, 76n, 77n, 81n, 98n, 106n, 114n, 116n
Foundations: assets of, 12; charters and deeds of trust of, 26–31, 70, 87, 88, 109; corporation, 11, 117; criticism of, 74–81, 85, 86, 92, 106; definition of, 11; difficulties in operation of, 111–113; effect of, 86, 113–115; essential ingredient, 5, 69–70; follow-up procedures of, 76–78; foreign activities of, 70–74, 122–125; future of, 69, 119; government regulation of, 102–105; historical background of, 15–19; investments of, 42, 43, 44, 118; liquidating, 27, 28; mistakes of, 53, 97, 106–111; motivation of, 15–25; need for, 113–117; optional, 27, 28; outside consultation of, 56–57, 60, 64, 70, 72–73; 93; perpetual, 26; programs of, 29, 52, 54–66; public accountability of,101–105; records, 57; relationship to higher education, 45, 52, 62; reporting of activities, by, 12, 68, 69, 81, 87, 97–101, 103, 108; statistical information regarding, 122–125; tax exemption of, 24–25, 67–70, 81–82, 88, 97, 99, 100, 102, 109, 116–117; types of, 11–12, 38–42, 67. *See also* Grants; Investigations
Foundations and Their Trends (Kopetzky), 75n
France, 19, 70
Frankenstein, 90
Franklin, Benjamin, 19
Fraud, prosecution for, 69, 78
Freedom of action, 5, 19, 67–74, 79–80, 85, 91, 104–105, 119
Fund for the Advancement of Education, The, 65
Funds and Foundations (Flexner), 21n, 48n, 109n
Funston, G. Keith, 115n

GAITHER, H. Rowan, Jr., 59, 101n
Galileo, 50
Geiger, Theodore, 117n
General Education Board: *Answers to Questionnaire*, 38n, 93n, 113n; creation of, 21, 22, 26; criticism of, 74; effect of, 113, 114; investments of, 43; program of, 55, 58, 63, 93; reports of, 55n, 63n, 81n; statistical information regarding, 123
Geographic limitations, 29, 34, 46, 64
Georgia, 92
Gildersleeve, Virginia C., 38
Girard, Stephen, 19
Glenn, John M., 21n, 81n
Goldthorpe, J. Harold, 56n
Gospel of Wealth, The (Carnegie), 22
Government: activities, 52, 91, 114, 115; consultation of foundations with, 60; foundation, 11, 118; foundation programs in, 82, 93; regulation of foundations, 48, 67–70, 87, 99, 102, 115; supplanting foundations, 115, 116, 117
Grantees, independence of, 40, 74–80, 107
Grants, 74, 83, 96, 97, 99, 107, 110, 118; classified, 38–42; follow-up procedure concerning, 76–78; objectivity in making of, 39; total number of, 54, 122–125. *See also* Foundations, foreign activities of
Gray, B. Kirkman, 46n
Greene, Jerome D., 87n
Guggenheim Memorial Foundation, John Simon, 18n, 41–42, 70, 123

HARKNESS family, 23
Harrison, Shelby M., 22n, 24n, 43, 61n
Hartford Foundation, John A., 30n, 123
Harvard Medical School, 75
Hayden Foundation, Charles, 31n, 123
Hays, Brooks, 6, 7, 13
Health, 29, 39, 71, 102
Hearings Before the Select (Cox) *Committee to Investigate Tax-Exempt Foundations and Comparable Organizations*, 12, 13n
Henry VIII, 18
Higgins Scientific Trust, Eugene, 30n, 123
Higher education, relationship of foundations to, 45, 52, 62
Higher Education, Philanthropy, and Federal Tax Exemption (Goldthorpe), 56n
Hill Family Foundation, Louis W. and Maud, 123
Hillquit, Morris, 86n

Hiss, Alger, 96
Hoffman, Paul G., 35*n*, 39*n*, 53*n*, 59*n*, 72, 73*n*, 94*n*, 100*n*, 111, 115*n*
Hollis, Ernest V., 15, 16*n*, 21*n*, 29*n*, 33*n*, 36*n*, 45*n*, 50, 56, 57*n*, 58*n*, 61*n*, 63*n*, 81, 89, 98, 113
Holmes, John Haynes, 86*n*
House Committee, on Un-American Activities, 96
Houston Endowment, 102, 123
Humanities, 42, 50, 52, 53, 60, 61, 107
Hurlin, Ralph G., 28*n*, 46*n*
Hutchins, Robert M., 53, 65*n*, 78*n*, 94*n*, 117*n*
Hyams Trust, Godfrey M., 30*n*, 123

IN *Defense of Scholarship* (Zinsser), 41*n*
"In the Service of Humanity" (Dodge), 51*n*
Income: average gross, 122–125; specifications as to expenditure of, 26–27
Incorporation by acts of Congress, 26, 123
India, 70
Industrial Relations: Final Report and Testimony Submitted to Congress (Senate Commission), 86*n*
Industrial Relations Commission Hearings of 1915, 6, 85–88
Infiltration, 96, 97
Institutional foundation, 38, 39, 40, 107
Insulin, discovery of, 109
Internal Revenue, Bureau of, 69, 100
Internal Revenue Code, 67, 68, 80, 82, 99, 102
International relations, 70–73, 82, 83
Investigations of foundations, congressional, 6, 7, 85–88, 92–97, 99, 127
Investment in People (Embree and Waxman), 27*n*, 42*n*
Investment policies, foundation, 42–44, 118
Italy, 50

JAMES Foundation of New York, 30*n*, 124
Johnson, Joseph E., 34*n*, 51*n*, 72*n*, 80, 94*n*, 100*n*
Juilliard Musical Foundation, 124
Julius Rosenwald Fund, 27, 57

KAISER Family Foundation, Henry J., 124
Keele, Harold M., 7, 13, 66*n*, 95
Kellogg Foundation, W. K., 71, 124

Keppel, Frederick P., 9*n*, 19, 21, 22*n*, 24*n*, 30*n*, 32, 35*n*, 36*n*, 40, 41, 42, 45, 51, 52*n*, 55, 57*n*, 60, 61, 63, 75, 76, 77*n*, 80, 81, 90, 97, 98*n*, 106*n*, 110, 114, 116*n*
Kiger, Joseph C., 6, 7
Kirchwey, George W., 86*n*
Kohlberg, Alfred M., 51*n*
Kopetzky, Samuel J., 75*n*
Kresge Foundation, 110*n*, 124

LADD Fund, Kate Macy, 30*n*, 124
Langland, William, 17
Laski, Harold, 107
Lasser, J. K., 24*n*
Lawson, John R., 86*n*
Leemon, Dorothy, 56*n*
Leffingwell, Russell C., 32*n*, 52, 53, 62, 94*n*, 111, 115*n*
Legislation, 67–70, 80–84, 99–105, 115–117; Internal Revenue Code, 67, 68, 80, 82, 99, 102; Statute of Charitable Uses, 18
Lester, Robert M., 13, 22*n*, 36*n*, 98*n*
Letters from Various Individuals Solicited by the Select Committee to Investigate Tax-Exempt Foundations and Comparable Organizations, 13, 115
Libbey Trust, Edward Drummond, 124
Library of Congress, 7, 13
Lilly Endowment, 83, 124
Lindeman, Eduard C., 23, 32, 61, 62, 75, 89, 98, 107, 108, 109
Loans, remedial, 81
Lobbying, attitude of foundations toward, 81, 83
Locale, limitations as to, 29, 34, 46, 64
"Ludlow massacre," 85

MACY Foundation, Josiah, Jr., 49*n*, 77*n*, 124
Manual of Corporate Giving, The (Ruml and Geiger), 117*n*
Markle Foundation, John and Mary R., 63*n*, 103, 124
Mayo Association, 30*n*, 124
McBride, Katharine, 115*n*
Medical Education in the United States and Canada (Flexner), 58*n*, 60, 109
Medical Society of the County of New York, 75
Medicine: cooperative research in, 40; fear of foundation control of, 75; foundation support of, 5, 6, 39, 60, 70, 82, 108; government support of, 50; systems of, 95

Mellon Educational and Charitable Trust, Andrew W., 30n, 42n, 124
Mexico, 70
Middlebush, Frederick, 52, 54n, 78n
Milbank Memorial Fund, 55n, 109, 112, 124
Miner Foundation, William H., 30n, 125
Missouri, University of, 52
"Modern Philanthropic Foundation: A Critique and a Proposal" (*Yale Law Journal*), 24n, 69n
Modern Philanthropy (Allen), 46n
Moe, Henry Allen, 18n, 42n, 106n, 110
Money to Burn (Coon), 43n
Motives of donors, 15–25
Mott Foundation, Charles Stewart, 125
Mullanphy Fund, 27
Myers, William I., 52n, 94n

NATIONAL Science Foundation, 11, 118
Natural sciences, 5, 6, 40, 50, 60, 61, 82, 114, 118
Nelson Trust, William Rockhill, 30n, 125
Nepotism, 35
Net worth, statistical information on, 122–125
New England, 34
New York, 29, 33, 34
New York Foundation, 125
New York Stock Exchange, 115

OBJECTIVITY, 39
Obsolescence, danger of, 27, 30, 31
Officers of foundations, 31–36, 59, 77, 91, 108, 118
Ogden, Robert C., 21
Ogg, Frederick A., 107n
Ohio, 29, 125
Old Dominion Foundation, 50, 84, 102, 125
Olin Foundation, 125
Operating foundations, 38, 39, 77, 107
Origin, statistical information on, 122–125
Orton, William A., 16n

PALLIATIVE giving, 46, 47, 48, 108, 111, 118
Pay for trustees, 34–35, 70
Peabody Education Fund, 20, 21
Peace, promotion of, 71, 72
Pension program, 63

"Perils of Magnanimity, The" (Zinsser), 75n
Perkins, George W., 87n
"Philanthropic Doubts" (Cannon), 47n, 89n
"Philanthropic Endowment in Modern Life, The" (Lester), 13, 36n, 98n
Philanthropic Foundations and Higher Education (Hollis), 21n, 29n, 33n, 36n, 45n, 56n, 57n, 58n, 61n, 63n, 81n, 89n
Philanthropic Giving (Andrews), 11, 26n, 28n
"Philanthropoids," 35
Philanthropy, dominant idea of modern, 46
Philanthropy and Learning (Keppel), 24n, 30n, 61n, 90n, 98n
Philanthropy and the State (Gray), 46n
Pickering, Danby, 18n
Pinchot, Amos, 86, 87n
"Place of Philanthropic Foundations in a Community, The" (Burns), 81n
Political activity, foundation, opposition to, 74, 81, 82, 83
Preventive venture-capital function of foundations: attitudes toward, 46–47, 67, 80, 108, 119; difficulties in application of, 85, 105; relative to foreign activity, 70–71; relative to programs, 54–55, 60–66. *See also* Venture capital
Principal, expenditure of, 26–27
"Principles of Public Giving" (Rosenwald), 27n
Pritchett, Henry S., 28, 51
"Private Fortunes and the Public Future" (Flexner), 91n
Programs, development of, 54–66, 108
Progress, philosophy of, 62
Progressive education, 65, 66, 89. *See also* Education
Propaganda, 68, 80–84
Prudent man, doctrine of, 43
Public Accountability of Foundations and Charitable Trusts (Taylor), 69n
Public administration, 82, 93
Public interest, affected with a, 81, 97
Public opinion, 53, 80–84, 87, 108
Public reporting, 12, 68, 69, 81, 87, 97–101, 103, 108
Public trust, 85–105, 108, 119

QUESTIONNAIRE, 10, 12, 127–137

REECE Committee, 6
Registry, public, 103
Relief, 46

Religion: control of foundations by, 69; influence in creation of foundations, 15–20, 24; support of, 50, 56, 64, 82, 102
Remuneration for trustees, 34–35, 70
Report of the Select Committee to Investigate Foundations and Other Organizations, Final, 92, 95, 96, 97, 101*n*, 119. *See also Hearings Before the Select Committee*
Report of the Study for the Ford Foundation on Policy and Program, 59*n*
Reporting, public, 12, 68, 69, 81, 87, 97–101, 103, 108
Research: basic, 54, 63, 64; cooperative, 40, 41; criticism of, 107, 109; economic, 93; foundation support of, 5, 49, 60, 82, 90, 93
Research in the Humanistic and Social Sciences (Ogg), 107*n*
Restrictive charters, 29, 30, 31
Revenue Code, Internal, 67–68, 80, 82
Rich, Wilmer Shields, 141
Risk capital. *See* Venture capital
Rockefeller Foundation: *Answers to Questionnaire*, 10*n*, 38*n*, 94*n*, 96*n;* creation of, 22; effect of, 10, 114; grants of, 96; investments of, 43, 44; officers of, 35, 100; operating practices, 37, 39, 46, 47, 48; program of, 55, 58, 60, 70, 71, 75, 85, 89, 94; reports of, 12, 44, 47*n*, 55*n*, 63*n*, 81*n*, 89, 90*n*, 97; statistical information regarding, 125; venture-capital concept of, 51, 60
Rockefeller Institute for Medical Research, 22
Rockefeller, John D., 21, 22, 37, 38, 46, 87*n*, 88
Rockefeller, John D., Jr., 87*n*
Rockefeller, John D., III, 94*n*
Rockefeller Memorial, Laura Spelman, 90*n*
Roman Catholic Church, 18
Rose, Milton C., 100*n*
Rose, Wickliffe, 21
Rosenberg Foundation, 125
Rosenwald, Julius, 27, 28, 111
Rosenwald Fund, Julius, 27, 57
Royal Commissions of Enquiry, 19
Ruml, Beardsley, 51, 117*n*
Rusk, Dean, 19*n*, 32*n*, 34*n*, 35*n*, 52*n*, 54*n*, 100*n*
Russell Sage Foundation, 6, 22, 81, 100, 103–104, 125
Russell Sage Foundation, 1907–1946 (Glenn, Brandt, Andrews), 21*n*, 81*n*
Russian Institute (Columbia University), 71

Sage, Mrs. Russell, 22
Sage Foundation, Russell, 6, 22, 81, 100, 103–104, 125
St. Louis, 27
"Scatteration giving," 39, 47, 48, 108, 109
Sciences: natural, 5, 6, 40, 50, 60, 61, 82, 114, 118; social, 5, 6, 42, 50, 52, 53, 60, 61, 82, 85, 86, 90, 93, 107, 115
Select Committee to Investigate Tax-Exempt Foundations and Comparable Organizations, 6, 7, 12, 13, 92. *See also Final Report; Hearings*
Senate Industrial Relations Commission of 1915, 5–6, 85–89
Senate Judiciary Committee, subcommittee of, 96–97
Seven Great Foundations (Ayres), 20
Seybold, Geneva, 61*n*
Simmons, James S., 51*n*
Simpson, Richard M., 13, 37, 80
Skeat, W. W., 17*n*
Slater Fund, 20, 21
Sloan, Alfred P., Jr., 32*n*, 51*n*, 54*n*, 94*n*, 95, 100*n*, 116*n*, 117
Sloan Foundation, Alfred P., 81*n*, 125
Smithson, James, 20
Smithsonian Institution, 20
Socialism, 92, 95
Social Science Research Council, 57, 60
Social sciences: attitudes toward, 53, 60, 61; foundation support of, 5, 6, 42, 50, 52, 82, 85, 86, 93, 107; government work in, 115; interpretation of, 91; necessity for research in, 90
Social welfare, 27, 60, 68
"Some Random Reminiscences of Men and Events" (Rockefeller), 38*n*
Southern Education Board, 21
Sparks, Frank H., 115*n*
Spelman Fund, 51
Spengler, Oswald, 62
Stanford University, 71
Statute of Charitable Uses, 18
Statutes at Large, The, 18*n*
Story of the Rockefeller Foundation, The (Fosdick), 21*n*, 39*n*, 47*n*, 63*n*
Straight, Michael Whitney, 32*n*, 37, 100*n*, 115*n*
"Subcontracting," 40
Subversion, 92, 93, 95, 96
Sugarman, Norman A., 69*n*, 99*n*
Surdna Foundation, 125

TAX boards and commissions, 68
Tax exemption, 24, 67–70, 72, 81–82, 88, 92, 97, 99, 100, 102, 109, 116–117
Taylor, Eleanor K., 69n
Texas, 29
"Timid Billions: Are the Foundations Doing Their Job?" (Embree), 33n
Timidity of foundations, 108
Toledo, Ohio, Museum of Art, 125n
Tolley, William B., 115n
"Trends Shown in the Establishment of Recent Foundations" (Hurlin), 28n, 46n
Trexler, Estate of Harry C., 82n, 125
"Triumphant Democracy" (Carnegie), 22
Trustees of foundations, 28, 31–36, 42, 59, 74, 87, 108, 111
Trusts: charitable, 5, 26, 68; community, 11, 108
Twentieth Century Fund, 50, 58, 79n, 93, 94n, 112, 125

UN-AMERICAN. See Subversion
United Nations, 72, 73, 80
United States Congress, 6, 9, 26, 85–88, 92, 95–96, 99, 127
United States Department of State, 72, 73
U.S. House of Representatives: Committee on Un-American Activities, 96; Select Committee to Investigate Foundations, 6, 7, 12, 13, 92
U.S. Senate: Industrial Relations Commission of 1915, 5, 6, 85–89; Subcommittee on Internal Security of the Judiciary Committee, 96–97

University of Alabama, 7
University of California, 60
University of Missouri, 52
University of Washington, 71
Untermeyer, Samuel, 87
"Use and Abuse of Endowments, The" (Pritchett), 28n

VANDERBILT University, 7
Venture capital, 49–66, 91, 110, 111, 112, 119. See also Preventive venture-capital function
Vincent, George E., 51
Vision of Piers the Plowman, The (Langland), 17, 18

WALSH, Frank P., 85
War, prevention of, 71
Washington, University of, 71
Washington University (St. Louis), 7
Waxman, Julia, 27n, 42n, 58n
Wealth and Culture (Lindeman), 23n, 32n, 61n, 75, 89n, 98n, 108n
Whitney Foundation, William C., 37
"Why Do So Many Business Men Start Foundations?" (Lasser), 24n
Wills of donors, 26
Wordsworth, William, 67
World War I, 50, 55, 59, 63, 80, 81, 89, 90
World War II, 24, 59, 90, 91
Wriston, Henry M., 65n, 66n, 78n, 94n, 95

YOUNG, Donald, 32n, 34n, 35n, 94n, 100

ZINSSER, Hans, 40, 41n, 75